Ba

AA

Munich

THE AUTOMOBILE ASSOCIATION

Imprint

Cover picture: Towers of the Frauenkirche

75 colour photographs
13 ground plans, 2 special plans, 1 transport plan (S-Bahn and U-Bahn), 1 city plan

Conception and editorial work:
Redaktionsbüro Harenberg, Schwerte

Text:
Johannes Kelch, Munich

General direction:
Dr Peter Baumgarten, Baedeker Stuttgart

Editorial work, English language:
Alec Court

Cartography:
Ingenieurbüro für Kartographie Huber & Oberländer, Munich

English translation:
James Hogarth

Source of illustrations:
Bavaria (1), Hetz (34), Historia-Photo (6), Mauritius (1), Messerschmidt (2), Prenzel (3), Reiter (19), Rudolph (3), Uthoff (6)

Following the tradition established by Karl Baedeker in 1844, sights of particular interest and hotels and restaurants of particular quality are distinguished by either one or two asterisks.

To make it easier to locate the various sights listed in the "A to Z" section of the Guide, their coordinates on the large city plan are shown in red at the head of each entry.

Only a selection of hotels and restaurants can be given: no reflection is implied, therefore, on establishments not included.

In a time of rapid change it is difficult to ensure that all the information given is entirely accurate and up to date, and the possibility of error can never be entirely eliminated. Although the publishers can accept no responsibility for inaccuracies and omissions, they are always grateful for corrections and suggestions for improvement.

1st English edition

Licensed user:
Mairs Geographischer Verlag GmbH & Co., Ostfildern-Kemnat bei Stuttgart

Reproductions:
Gölz Repro-Service GmbH, Ludwigsburg

The name *Baedeker* is a registered trademark

Printed in Great Britain by Jarrold and Sons Ltd, Norwich

ISBN 086145 326 3

Contents

Preface

This Pocket Guide to Munich is one of the new generation of Baedeker guides.

Baedeker pocket guides, illustrated throughout in colour, are designed to meet the needs of the modern traveller. They are quick and easy to consult, with the principal features of interest described in alphabetical order and practical details about location, opening times, etc., shown in the margin.

Each city guide is divided into three parts. The first part gives a general account of the city, its history, notable personalities and so on; in the second part the principal sights are described; and the third part contains a variety of practical information designed to help visitors to find their way about and make the most of their stay.

The Baedeker pocket guides are noted for their concentration on essentials and their convenience of use. They contain numerous specially drawn plans and coloured illustrations, and in a pocket at the back of the book is a large plan of the city. Each entry in the main part of the guide gives the coordinates of the square on the plan in which the particular feature can be located. Users of this guide, therefore, will have no difficulty in finding what they want to see.

Facts and Figures

Munich's coat of arms

General

Munich (in German München) is capital of the *Land* (province) of Bavaria (Bayern), one of the ten *Länder* that make up the Federal Republic of Germany. The third-largest German city, it is sometimes called the "secret capital of Germany".

Geographical situation

Munich lies in South Germany on the so-called Munich Inclined Plane, an area (1485 sq. km (573 sq. miles)) of sloping gravel terraces deposited by Ice Age glaciers and inundated by the River Isar, which flows through the city from south to north for some 14 km (9 miles). The land lies at an average height of 530 m (1740 ft) above sea-level, ranging from 480 m (1575 ft) at the lowest point to 580 m (1905 ft) at the highest.
To the north of Munich the gravel plain gives place to the Dachauer and Erdinger Moos (Moss); to the south extends the morainic landscape of the Alpine foreland. The chain of the Alps is some 40–60 km (25–40 miles) south of the city as the crow flies.

Telephone dialling code

From the United Kingdom: 010 49 89
From the United States or Canada: 011 49 89

Area and population

Munich covers an area of 311 sq. km (120 sq. miles), its greatest length being 26 km (16 miles), its greatest breadth 21 km (13 miles). The conurbation which has grown up round Munich extends for some 10 km (6 miles) beyond the city boundaries. The city's population is 1·3 million, of whom only some 32 per cent are natives of Munich and 16 per cent are foreigners. Since the 1970s the area available within the city for industry, commerce and housing has been found to be inadequate, and there have been moves to extend its boundaries by taking in adjoining communes. The last expansions of this kind took place during the Nazi period and were carried through against the wishes of the population.

Administrative divisions

For administrative purposes the city is divided into 41 wards (*bezirke*). Since the names of the wards are not all in common use, only the names of the generally recognised districts within the city are given here.
The central area (Innenstadt) takes in the Altstadt (Old Town), Maxvorstadt and Isarvorstadt, Lehel and the Wiesen district; to the north are Schwabing, Freimann, Milbertshofen-Hart and Feldmoching; to the east Bogenhausen, Haidhausen, Au, Giesing, Harlaching, Berg am Laim, Trudering, Ramersdorf and Perlach; to the south Sendling, Thalkirchen, Fürstenried, Solin, the Waldfriedhof district and Hadern; to the west Schwanthalerhöhe (Westend), Laim, Pasing, Aubing, Neuhausen, Obermenzing, Untermenzing, Allach and Langwied.

◀ *New Town Hall, Marienplatz*

Those areas of the city which were developed in the 19th c. and are now in need of modernisation, including the Maxvorstadt and Isarvorstadt, Schwabing, Lehel, Au and Neuhausen, are in process of being improved and rehabilitated. Although there has been a housing shortage in Munich since the end of the 1970s, house-building in the city is at present stagnating.

Administration

Munich is governed by a directly elected Chief Burgomaster, two burgomasters appointed by the city council (Stadtrat) and twelve councillors, each responsible for a particular department. The Chief Burgomaster is the city's chief officer and representative and head of the administration. The municipal parliament (Stadtparlament) consists of 80 councillors (unpaid), who sit both in plenary session and in committee.
The burgomasters and councillors serve for a six-year term.

Population and Religion

Statistically the population of Munich shows a slight declining trend, but since there is a continuing movement of population into the Munich region the number of people living and working in the conurbation continues to increase.

Religion

Some two-thirds of the population are Catholics and just under a third are Protestants; the city has 117 Catholic and 63 Protestant parishes. There are 4000 Jews, with two synagogues, and 13,000 Muslims, with one mosque.

Transport

Air transport

Munich's commercial airport, München-Riem, lies 8 km (5 miles) east of the city centre on B 12 (airport bus from Central Station every 20 minutes). With a runway 2804m (3067 yd) long and 60 m (65 yd) wide, it provides direct connections with the main European capitals and links with the international network of air services.
In terms of passengers handled, Munich airport takes third place in Germany (5·9 million passengers annually, over 460 aircraft movements daily).
It is planned to establish a new and larger airport in the Erdinger Moos. Work began in November 1980 but was suspended soon afterwards following a court injunction.

Rail transport

Munich is a major centre of international, national and regional rail transport, with through services to the principal European capitals.

Local traffic

Munich's U-Bahn (Underground), S-Bahn (Suburban rail system), trams and almost all buses are combined and coordinated in the Münchner Verkehrs- und Tarifverbund or MVV (Transport and Tariff Combine).
The U-Bahn system is planned to reach a total length of over 90 km (55 miles). The first line (U 6), brought into use in 1971, runs in a north–south direction, intersecting with the S-Bahn in the Marienplatz. The Olympic Line (U 3) to the Olympic Centre (Olympiazentrum) was opened in time for the Summer Olympics of 1972. A line from the Olympic Centre via the

Murals in Königsplatz U-Bahn station

Central Station to Perlach (U 8) came into service in 1980; and two further lines (U 1 West from the Central Station to Rotkreuzplatz and U 6 West to the West Park, venue of the International Garden Show) were completed in 1983. Another line (U 5/9) from Schwanthalerhöhe (Westend) via the city centre to Arabella Park, Bogenhausen, is at present in course of planning and construction.

The S-Bahn system, which serves all parts of the Munich region, has a total length of some 410 km (255 miles). At the centre of the network is a 4·2 km (2·6 mile) long section which runs in a tunnel from the Central Station to the East Station, cutting across the Altstadt (Old Town) and connecting with the U-Bahn (Marienplatz, Hauptbahnhof) and the tramway system (Stachus). Of the 135 S-Bahn stations 40 are in Munich itself. Further developments are in progress.

Motorways

Munich can be reached from any direction by motorway (*autobahn*):

A 8: Stuttgart and the west (E 11)
A 8: Salzburg and the east (E 11); connection with Brenner motorway into Italy
A 9: Nürnberg and the north (E 6)
A 95: Garmisch-Partenkirchen and the south (E 6); branch (A 952) to Starnberg
A 96: Gilching-Unterpfaffenhofen (E 61) to the Ammersee
A 99: section of ring motorway; connections with Nürnberg and Salzburg motorway

Federal highways

Federal highways (*Bundesstrassen*) serving Munich:

B 2: Fürstenfeldbruck–Augsburg

B 2:Weilheim–Garmisch-Partenkirchen
B 11:Freising–Landshut–Deggendorf
B 12:Landsberg–Memmingen
B 12:Mühldorf–Passau
B 13:Bad Tölz–Sylvensteinspeicher
B 304:Wasserburg–Traunstein–Salzburg

Culture

General

Munich has some 35 theatres (including four state theatres), with a total of over 11,000 seats (excluding cabarets, etc.), 30 museums, galleries and collections, many of them world-famed, 75 cinemas with an annual audience of some 6 million, four symphony orchestras (Munich Philharmonic, Bavarian State Orchestra, Radio Symphony Orchestra, Graunke Symphony Orchestra) and several chamber orchestras and choirs. Its nine universities and institutes of higher education have a total of some 85,000 students. The largest of its numerous libraries is the Bavarian State Library, with some 4·8 million volumes and manuscripts.

Universities, etc.

The Ludwig Maximilian University, with some 50,000 students, is Germany's second largest university, exceeded in size only by the Free University in Berlin. It was founded in Ingolstadt in 1472 by Duke Ludwig IX and transferred to Landshut in 1800 by Elector Maximilian IV Joseph, and then to Munich in 1826 by King Ludwig I. The large and imposing University building, in Romanesque style, was built by

The National Theatre, in neo-classical style

Fountain in front of the University, with the Ludwigskirche in the background

Friedrich von Gärtner in 1835–40 and later much enlarged. It stands in Geschwister-Scholl-Platz, the Forum der Wissenschaften (Forum of Learning), just off the Ludwigstrasse.
The University of Technology (Technische Universität) was founded in 1863 as the Technical College of Engineering, Surveying, Architecture and Agriculture, an amalgamation of earlier technical schools. Professors who have taught here include the architects Friedrich Thiersch and Theodor Fischer, the chemist Hans Fischer (Nobel Prize 1930), the engineer Carl von Linde and the physicist Werner Heisenberg. Many research institutes attached to the University of Technology have moved out to Garching, 13 km (8 miles) north of Munich.
Munich's smallest institute of higher education is the Film and Television College (Hochschule für Film und Fernsehen), which has something over 100 students.

Academies

The Academy of Art (Akademie der Bildenen Künste) has classes in painting, the graphic arts, sculpture, art education, etc., with some 700 students. The Bavarian Academy of Sciences (Akademie der Wissenschaften) and Academy of Fine Arts (Akademie der Schönen Künste) admit only scientists or artists whose work shows particular merit.

Scientific societies and institutes

Among Munich's numerous public and private scientific research institutes are the Max Planck Society for the Promotion of Science, with institutes of biochemistry, physics, phychiatry and psychopathology; the Fraunhofer Society for the Promotion of Applied Research, with institutes of natural science and technology; and the Society for Radiation and Environmental Research, which carries on ecological and medical research.

Commerce and Industry

General

In 1980 Munich's economy had a total turnover worth 151 billion DM (without Value Added Tax), of which industry and craft production accounted for 70 billion. In that year the city had a working population of 775,000 (including the self-employed), of whom 178,000 were in the processing industries, 120,000 in trade and 160,000 in the public service (including public corporations).

Industry

Among the industrial cities of the Federal Republic Munich takes third place, after Berlin and Hamburg (measured by the number of firms and the number in employment). The principal branches of industry are mechanical engineering and vehicle production, the optical industry, electrical engineering and the foodstuffs industries. Among the largest and best-known firms are Krauss-Maffei, the Bayerische Motorenwerke (BMW), Messerschmitt-Bölkow-Blohm, MAN, the Rodenstock optical works, Siemens (the largest private firm in Munich) and the six large breweries which produce more than 4·5 million hectolitres (99 million gallons) of beer annually (Augustinerbräu, Hacker & Pschorr, Hofbräu, Löwenbräu, Paulanerbräu and Spatenbräu).
Munich is Germany's principal publishing centre, with 300 publishing houses.

Trade fairs

At the beginning of the 20th c. an exhibition ground for trade fairs, with facilities for congresses as well as exhibition halls, was laid out in the Bavaria Park on the Theresienhöhe. The trade fair complex was badly damaged during the Second World War, and new buildings, carefully designed for their purpose, were erected after the war. Some 20 trade fairs and exhibitions and 40 congresses and conferences are held here every year; in 1980 there was a total of 1·7 million visitors.
The Bayernhalle (3500 seats), Kongresshalle (850 seats), Messehaus (220 seats) and various other halls provide excellent facilities for congresses, conferences and events connected with trade fairs.
Among trade fairs regularly held here are BAUMA (constructional machinery), CARAVAN + BOOT/INTERNATIONALER REISEMARKT (International Travel Market), COSMETICS, IHM (crafts), INTERBRAU (brewing), INHORGENTA, ISPO, MODEWOCHE MÜNCHEN (fashion), PRODUKTRONICA, SYSTEMS (computer systems), TRANSPORT and VISODATA (media systems).

Banking and insurance

The Bayerische Hypotheken- und Wechselbank and Bayerische Vereinsbank are two of the "big five" banks of the Federal Republic. About a hundred insurance companies have offices in Munich, including the Münchener Rückversicherung (Munich Reinsurance Corporation), the largest institution of its kind in Europe, and the Allianz, Europe's largest direct insurers.

Tourism

Munich has some 350 hotels and guest-houses with a total of 25,000 beds. The number of visitor-nights in 1982 was about 5 million.

Commerce

As early as the 15th c. Munich was the meeting-place of trade routes running from west to east and from north to south. In our own time its Central Market is a major centre of trade in fruit and vegetables from the countries to the south and south-east (handling just under 1 million tonnes in 1982); and Munich vies with Hamburg as the largest market for livestock and meat in the Federal Republic.

Stock Exchange

The Bavarian Stock Exchange (visitor service Mon.–Fri. 11.30 a.m.–1.30 p.m.) developed out of the Merchants' Chamber (Kaufmannsstube) founded in 1829.

Notable Personalities

Duke Albert (Albrecht) V (1528–79)

Duke Albert V, the Magnanimous, succeeded his brother as Duke in 1550. A resolute opponent of the Reformation, he summoned the Jesuits to Munich in order to strengthen the Catholic faith in the city. With his Kunstkammer (Cabinet of Curios) and Antiquarium (see A to Z, Residence), the first museums in Germany, he established Munich's reputation as a city of art and culture.

Egid Quirin Asam (1692–1750)

Cosmas Damian Asam (1686–1739)

the Asam brothers – Egid Quirin, sculptor, stucco artist, painter and architect, and Cosmas Damian, painter and architect – were the founders and principal representatives of the Bavarian Rococo school.
Both studied in Rome and were influenced by Bernini, and between them they created the interiors of many Munich churches – the Church of the Holy Ghost, the two churches of St Anne, the Trinity Church, the Asam Church and St Mary's in Thalkirchen.
Visitors to Munich can still see the house occupied by Egid Quirin Asam, with his rich stucco ornament on the façade (see A to Z, Asam House).

François de Cuvilliés the Elder (1695–1768)

François de Cuvilliés, a native of Hainaut (which then belonged to Austria) and a dwarf – indeed he started his career as Duke Maximilian Emanuel's Court Dwarf – was the greatest architect and interior decorator of the South German Rococo. After receiving a thorough training in Paris he became Court Architect in Munich in 1725. His principal works are the Cuvilliés Theatre, the Rich Apartments in the Residence, the Amalienburg and the façade of the Theatinerkirche. His son François de Cuvilliés the Younger was also an architect in Munich.

Georges Desmarées (1697–1776)

Georges Desmarées or Marées, born in Sweden, the son of a French *émigré*, was the principal representative of French Rococo portrait-painting in Munich. After training in Amsterdam, Nürnberg and Venice he became Bavarian Court Painter in 1730. Examples of his work are to be seen in the Residence, Schleissheim and Nymphenburg palaces, the Amalienburg, the Municipal Gallery, the National Museum and the Alte Pinakothek.

Notable Personalities

Joseph Effner (1687–1745)	After studying architecture and landscape architecture in Paris Joseph Effner, a native of Dachau, became Court Architect in Munich in 1715 (a post in which he was succeeded by Cuvilliés). He was responsible for the enlargement of Nymphenburg Palace to its present size, built the Badenburg, Pagodenburg and Magdalenenklause in Nymphenburg Park and designed the extensions to Schleissheim New Palace. Fürstenried Castle and the Preysing-Palais were also his work.
Johann Michael Fischer (1692–1766)	The architect Johann Michael Fischer was one of the creators and the most important representative of the Bavarian Rococo. He developed the idea of the centralised plan which played such a dominant part in Rococo church architecture. Altogether he built 32 churches and 23 religious houses in Bavaria. In Munich itslef he was responsible for St Anne's Church in Sankt-Anna-Platz (the very first Rococo church) and St Michael's in Berg am Laim.
Karl von Fischer (1782–1820)	Karl von Fischer, a sensitive neo-classical architect, was summoned by King Ludwig I from Mannheim, where he had acquired some reputation, to Munich. There he built 36 public and private buildings, most of them now destroyed. Among those which have survived or been restored are the National Theatre and Prinz-Carl-Palais. In association with Ludwig von Sckell, Fischer prepared the plan for the 19th c. extension of Munich.
Joseph von Fraunhofer (1787–1826)	Joseph von Fraunhofer, a native of Straubing, was trained as a glass-grinder and mirror-maker. From 1809 he worked as an optician and physicist (without academic training) in Munich, where he published the results of his pioneering experiments (the Fraunhofer lines) in 1814. He also developed a number of important optical instruments. He was one of the first to put into practice the new idea of basing production processes on scientific theories. His workshop has been reconstructed in its original form in Munich's Municipal Museum.
Friedrich von Gärtner (1792–1847)	Friedrich von Gärtner was trained as an architect in Munich, and after a study tour in Italy, where he became familiar with the forms of classical architecture, he succeeded Leo von Klenze as architect responsible for the development of the Ludwigstrasse in 1827 (though officially appointed only in 1832). An architect of the Romantic/Christian school, he achieved a synthesis of neo-classical principles of proportion and historical forms (Romanesque, Byzantine, Gothic, Renaissance). His principal works in Munich were the State Library, the Ludwigskirche, the University, the Feldherrnhalle and the Siegestor.
Hubert Gerhard (*c.* 1550–1620)	After a period of training under Giovanni da Bologna in Florence Hubert Gerhard worked as a sculptor in bronze in Augsburg, Munich and Innsbruck. As the principal representative of the South German school of bronze sculpture about 1600 he played a major part in the development of sculpture from Mannerism to Early Baroque. He created the figure of St Michael and the dragon on the façade of St Michael's Church and the figure of the Virgin as Patroness of Bavaria on the Mariensäule in the Marienplatz.

Joseph von Fraunhofer

Leo von Klenze

Franz von Lenbach

Erasmus Grasser
(*c.* 1450–after 1526)

The sculptor and woodcarver Erasmus Grasser came to Munich about 1474. He carved 16 figures of Morisco dancers for the Council Chamber of the Old Town Hall in Munich (now in the Municipal Museum).

Ignaz Günther
(1725–75)

The sculptor Ignaz Günther, a native of the Upper Palatintate, became a pupil of Johann Baptist Straub and in 1754 set up his own studio in Munich (see A to Z, Ignaz Günther's House). His figures are elegant, elaborate, somewhat artificial creations of considerable dramatic effect. His work is the very peak and perfection of Rococo sculpture. Examples can be seen in the Frauenkirche, the Bürgersaal, St Peter's Church, the Asam Church, St George's in Bogenhausen, St Mary's in Thalkirchen, Schleissheim New Palace and the Bavarian National Museum.

Wassily Kandinsky
(1866–1944)

The Russian painter Wassily Kandinsky, one of the founders of abstract art, began by studying law in Moscow but soon devoted himself entirely to art. After travelling in Tunisia, Italy and France he came to Munich in 1896 and worked there (with interruptions) until 1918. A pupil of Franz von Stuck, he became President of the New Artists' Union (Neue Künstler-vereinigung) in 1907, and in 1910 painted his first abstract picture. In 1911, with Franz Marc, he founded the Blauer Reiter (Blue Rider) group.
The Municipal Gallery's Kandinsky Collection (see A to Z, Lenbach Villa) comprises some 500 works of Kandinsky's Munich period.

Leo von Klenze
(1784–1864)

Leo von Klenze displaced Karl von Fischer as the royal Master of Works in 1816. The numerous buildings he designed, in strict neo-classical style, left his distinctive stamp on the townscape of Munich in the first half of the 19th c.: the Leuchtenberg-Palais, the Basargebäude (Bazaar), the southern section of the Ludwigstrasse, the Glyptothek, the Alte Pinakothek, the Königsbau and Festsaaltrakt of the Residence, the Propylaea and the Hall of Fame. Klenze was also a painter, draughtsman and writer.

Hans Krumper
(*c.* 1570–1634)

Hans Krumper, a native of Weilheim in Upper Bavaria and a pupil of Hubert Gerhard, worked at the Bavarian Court as sculptor in bronze, interior decorator and architect from 1592.

Influenced by Dutch and Italian Mannerism, he played a major part in the development of an independent school of Early Baroque sculpture in southern Germany. His principal works were the figure of the Virgin as the Patroness of Bavaria on the façade of the Residence, the Wittelsbach Fountain in the Residence, the Tomb of Emperor Ludwig the Bavarian in the Frauenkirche and the Temple in the Hofgarten.

Franz von Lenbach
(1836–1904)

Franz von Lenbach, as the leading portrait-painter of the Gründerzeit (the period of rapid economic development in the early 1870s), was a dominant figure in the artistic life of Munich in the latter part of the 19th c. His palatial villa now houses the Municipal Gallery (see A to Z, Lenbach Villa).

Franz Marc
(1880–1916)

The Expressionist painter Franz Marc, a native of Munich, founded with Kandinsky the Blauer Reiter (Blue Rider) group in 1911. There are some of his famous animal pictures in the Municipal Gallery (see A to Z, Lenbach Villa).

Oskar von Miller
(1855–1934)

The Munich engineer Oskar von Miller was a pioneering discoverer and organiser in the field of power production (Walchensee hydroelectric station, Bayernwerk power station). In 1882 he achieved the first transmission of electric power in the world (from Miesback to Munich). In 1903 he founded the German Museum.

Jan Polack
(*c.* 1435–1519)

A native of Cracow, Jan Polack came to Munich about 1470 and became Municipal Painter, painting numerous frescoes and altar-pieces. He ranks as the most important Munich painter of the Late Gothic period. Among his surviving works are the paintings for the old High Altar of St Peter's Church, the altar-pieces in the Chapel of Blutenberg Castle and the wall-paintings in the Pippinger Kircherl.

Ludwig von Schwanthaler
(1802–48)

Ludwig von Schwanthaler, a sculptor of the Romantic/neo-classical school, enjoyed the patronage of King Ludwig !, and in 1835 became Professor of Sculpture in Munich. He created numerous colossal statues and designed frescoes and reliefs for Ludwig I's apartments in the Königsbau of the Residence. His best-known work is the statue of Bavaria on the Theresienhöhe.

Carl Spitzweg
(1808–85)

Carl Spitzweg, a native of Munich, was originally a pharmacist, but taught himself to paint and in 1836 became a member of the Munich Artists' Union. He painted landscapes, but he is best known for the pictures in which he depicted, with irony and mockery, the foolishness, naïvety and narrow-mindedness of the good Munich townspeople of his day and the serene world of the Biedermeier period. In 1840 he began to work as an illustrator for the humorous journal "Fliegende Blätter". One of his best-known paintings, "The Poor Poet", is in the Neue Pinakothek.

Johann Baptist Straub
(1704–84)

Johann Baptist Straub became Court Sculptor in Munich in 1737. His principal works in Munich are in the Trinity Church, All Saints Church at the Cross, St Anne's Church in Sankt-Anna-Platz, St Michael's Church in Berg am Laim, the Cuvilliés Theatre and Nymphenburg Palace and Park. He also did work for the abbeys of Schäftlarn and Ettal.

Oskar von Miller

Carl Spitzweg

Richard Strauss

Richard Strauss
(1864–1949)

The composer and conductor Richard Strauss, one of the leading representatives of the German Late Romantic school, was born in a house at the Altheimer Eck in the old town of Munich. His father was as horn-player in the Court Orchestra, his mother a daughter of the Pschorr brewing family. After the failure of his first opera, "Guntram", none of his other works received their first performance in Munich until 1938. He is commemorated by a fountain in Neuhauser Strasse (pedestrian zone).

Franz von Stuck
(1863–1928)

A rival of Franz von Lenbach, Franz von Stuck was one of the founders of the Munich "Secession" group in 1892 and became one of the most influential and most versatile of Art Nouveau artists. Starting as a graphic artist (caricatures, posters), he came under the influence of Böcklin and created in his pictures a fantastic imaginary world of mythological and symbolic figures. His villa in Prinzregentenstrasse is now an Art Nouveau Museum (see A to Z, Stuck Villa).

Friedrich Sustris
(*c.* 1540–1599)

Born in Italy, the son of a Flemish painter, Sustris brought Dutch and Italian Mannerism to Munich, where he worked as a painter, decorator and architect. In 1580 he became "Artistic Director" at the Court of Duke William V. He designed the Grottenhof (Grotto Court) in the Residence and the Jesuit college now known as the Old Academy, and played an important part in the construction of St Michael's Church.

Ludwig Thoma
(1867–1921)

Ludwig Thoma was originally a lawyer, but in 1899 he became Editor of the satirical journal "Simplicissimus", a post which he held until his death. He was also a prolific writer. In 1907, together with Hermann Hesse, he founded "März", a journal directed against "life in the great cities".
The best known of his numerous humorous and satirical works (poems, novels, short stories) are "Lausbubengeschichten" (1905), "Erste Klasse" (a farce, 1910) and "Jozef Filsers Briefwexel" (1912). His comedies and satirical one-act plays, "Die Medaille" (1901), "Die Lokalbahn" (1902) and "Moral" (1909), made a major contribution to the development of comedy in the early years of the 20th c.

Enrico Zuccalli
(*c.* 1642–1724)

Enrico Zuccalli, a native of the Grisons (Switzerland), ranks with Viscardi and Barelli as one of the principal representatives of Italian Baroque in Bavaria. Appointed Court Architect in Munich in 1673, he completed the Theatinerkirche and from 1680 onwards played a major part in the decoration of the Residence.
Among his other works were Lustheim Palace, Schleissheim New Palace and the Palais Porcia (later altered by Cuvilliés).

History of Munich

4000 B.C.
First evidence of human settlement.

500–15 B.C.
Celtic settlement.

From A.D. 530
Bavarian settlement in the Munich area (hence place-names ending in -ing, like Pasing, Sendling, Schwabing and Aubing, all now districts in Munich).

10th–11th c.
Monks from Tegernsee settle on the banks of the Isar, establishing a village which becomes known as "Munichen" ("at the monks' place"). The origin of the town is still recalled in Munich's coat of arms, which depicts a monk in a black habit edged with gold.

1158
Foundation of a town by the Guelf Duke Henry the Lion. The Duke of Saxony and Bavaria destroys the Bishop of Freising's toll-bridge, downstream from the town, builds a bridge, market and mint at the monkish settlement of Munichen and protects them with a circuit of walls.

1180
Henry the Lion outlawed by the Emperor. Bavaria passes into the hands of the Wittelsbachs.

1255
Munich becomes the Wittelsbachs' capital.

14th c.
(first half)
Munich becomes the residence of the Emperor Ludwig the Bavarian. The town grows to five times its original size and is surrounded by a second ring of walls.

1632
Munich is occupied by Gustavus Adolphus of Sweden during the Thirty Years War.

1634
A third of the population (some 7000 people) carried off by plague.

1704–14
Munich is occupied by Austrian troops during the War of the Spanish Succession.

1705
A rising by Bavarian peasants is bloodily repressed just outside Munich.

1791
The town walls, which hamper the growth of the town, are pulled down.

1806
Establishment of the kingdom of Bavaria. Munich becomes capital of a much enlarged state, with a rigidly centralised

government. In the following decades large-scale extensions of the town take place, the Maxvorstadt, Ludwigsvorstadt and Isarvorstadt districts are developed, magnificent neo-classical buildings and museums are erected, adjoining communes are incorporated in the town. Munich becomes known as a city of art and culture.

First International Industrial Exhibition in Munich. — 1854

The wave of industrialisation does not reach Munich until about the turn of the century. It brings with it a massive influx of population from rural areas. New suburban districts come into being (Haidhausen). Many churches are built in "historical" styles. — 19th c. (second half)

The November Revolution, led by Kurt Eisner, begins in Bavaria. Proclamation of a Free State. — November 1918

The anarchist, and later Communist, Räterepublik (*räte*= councils, soviets) is ruthlessly repressed by the Reichswehr in April and May. — Spring 1919

A National Socialist *putsch*, the "March to the Feldherrnhalle", is defeated. — November 1923

About half the buildings in Munich are destroyed in 1944–45 by 60,000 explosive bombs and 50,000 incendiary bombs. Over 22,000 Munich soldiers and more than 6500 inhabitants lose their lives. — 1939–45

The population of Munich reaches the million mark. Satellite towns (e.g. Neuperlach) are developed during the 1960s and 1970s. — 1957

In preparation for the Olympic Games a new U-Bahn (Underground) and S-Bahn (Suburban) system is established. A pedestrian zone is created in the city centre. — 1971–72

20th Summer Olympic Games in Munich. Arab terrorists attack the Israeli team in the Olympic Village, taking hostages; an attempt to free them on Fürstenfeldbruck military airfield fails, and altogether 11 Israeli athletes are killed. — 1972

New galleries of Neue Pinakothek opened. — 1981

Munich's 825th birthday. – 4th International Garden Show (IGA 83). – Further sections of U-Bahn brought into use. — 1983

Sights from A to Z

Academy of Art (Akademie der Bildenden Künste) M18

Location
Akademiestrasse 2

U-Bahn
Universität

The Academy of Art, which provides training in painting, graphic art, sculpture and art education, lies just at the Siegestor (see entry).
This long range of buildings (230m (755 ft) in length) with projecting wings was built between 1874 and 1885 by Gottfried von Neureuther in the style of the Italian High Renaissance. In a manner characteristic of the architecture of the Gründerzeit (the period of rapid industrial expansion in the early 1870s) the design is concerned only to achieve an effect of imposing grandeur on the main (south) front.

All Saints Church at the Cross (Allerheiligenkirche am Kreuz) O17

Location
Kreuzstrasse 10

U-Bahn
Sendlinger-Tor-Platz

S-Bahn
Karlsplatz, Marienplatz

All Saints, formerly the cemetery church of St Peter's parish, was built about 1478 by Jörg von Halspach (known as Ganghofer), architect of the Frauenkirche. Secularised after the closing of the cemetry in 1789, it is now the church of Munich's Ukrainian Catholics.
This Gothic church, oriented to the south, is built of brick without plaster or other facing. The semicircular apse (chancel) dates from the Baroque remodelling of the church in 1620.
Notable features of the interior: painting on the High Altar, "The Virgin appearing to St Augustine", by Johann Rottenhammer (17th c.); tabernacle of the school of J. B. Straub (1770); fragment of a Gothic fresco of Christ in a mandorla above the east doorway (now walled up); wooden Crucifix by Hans Leinberger (1520) above west doorway; monument ("Raising of Lazarus") to the banker Goetz by Hans Krumper (1627).

Almeida Palace (Almeida-Palais) N18

Location
Brienner Strasse 14

U-Bahn
Odeonsplatz

S-Bahn
Karlsplatz

This mansion in strict neo-classical style (now the offices of a fire insurance company), designed by Jean-Baptiste Métivier, a pupil of Leo von Klenze, is a typical example of the original architectural style of the Brienner Strasse. It was built for Sophie Petin, who was granted the title of Baroness von Bayrstorff in 1823 and married her lover Prince Carl, Ludwig I's brother, in 1834. Count d'Almeida was her son-in-law.

Alte Akademie

See Old Academy

Rubens Room, Alte Pinakothek

**Alte Pinakothek (Old Picture Gallery) N17/18

The Alte Pinakothek, one of the world's largest and finest picture galleries, was built by Leo von Klenze between 1826 and 1836, replacing the older gallery by the Hofgarten, which had become too small for the steadily increasing Royal Collection. It was so badly damaged by air attack in 1944–45 that demolition was contemplated; but between 1953 and 1963 it was restored, and the gallery's treasures, which had been stored in places of safety, could again be put on display. This "masterpiece of architectural proportion" (Wölfflin) is modelled on the Renaissance palaces of Venice. The largest gallery built in the first half of the 19th c., it became the model for other galleries in Rome, Brussels and Kassel. It is a massive structure 127 m (417 ft) long with short side wings (37 m (121 ft) from front to back). The 24 statues (by Ludwig Schwanthaler) of famous painters on the south front and the frescoes (by Peter Cornelius) in the interior were destroyed by wartime bombing. Renovation work was carried out in the late 1970s.

All European schools of painting from the Middle Ages to the beginning of the 19th c. are represented in the Alte Pinakothek. The nucleus of the collection was a series of historical pictures painted for Duke William IV of Bavaria about 1530. The famous pictures by Dürer were acquired by Elector Maximilian I (1623–51). During the 18th c. valuable collections were acquired from Düsseldorf, Mannheim and Zweibrücken, including works by French and Dutch painters (Rubens, Van Dyck). Altar-pieces came from secularised churches and religious houses. The collection was also extended by purchases in the 19th and 20th c.

Location
Barer Strasse 27

U-Bahn
Theresienstrasse,
Königsplatz

Opening times
Tue.–Sun. 9 a.m.–4.30 p.m.; also 7–9 p.m. Tue. and Thu.

Conducted tours
Thu. 7.15 p.m. (enquire)

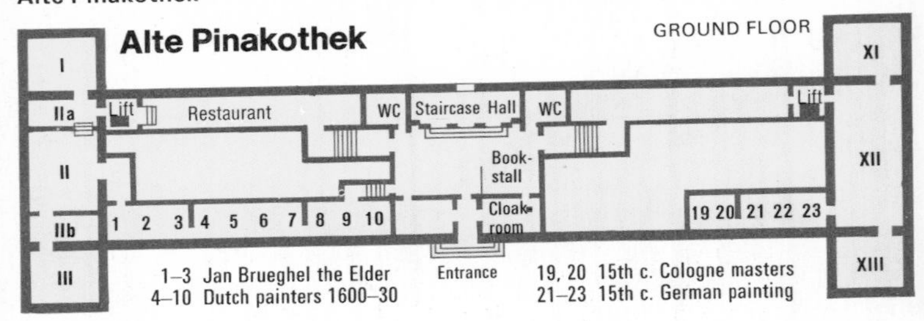

I Dutch painters 1530–60
IIa Brueghel the Elder

II German painting after 1530
IIb Elsheimer
III Dutch painters about 1600

XI Pacher
XII Holbein the Elder
XIII Cologne masters

Notable works

A selection of the most notable works:

South German painters of the 15th and 16th c.:
Altdorfer, "Alexander's Battle"
Baldung-Grien, "Nativity"
Cranach the Elder, "Christ on the Cross"
Dürer, "The Four Apostles"
Grünewald, "SS. Erasmus and Maurice"
Holbein, Altar of St Sebastian
Pacher, Altar of the Fathers of the Church
Schongauer, "Holy Family"

Early Dutch and Flemish painters and painters of the Lower Rhineland, 15th and 16th c.:
Bouts the Younger, winged altar, the "Pearl of Brabant"
Brueghel the Elder, "Land of Cockayne"
Master of the Life of Mary
Roger van der Weyden, Altar of the Three Kings

Flemish painters of the late 16th and 17th c.:
Brouwer, small genre paintings
Van Dyck, "Youthful Self-Portrait"
Van Dyck, "Rest on the Flight"
Rubens, "Battle of the Amazons", "Drunken Silenus", "Last Judgment", "Fall of the Damned", "Rubens and Isabella Brant [his first wife] in the Honeysuckle Arbour", "Lion-Hunt"

Dutch painters, end of 16th c. to 18th c.:
Rembrandt, "Self-Portrait as a Young Man", "Holy Family in the Carpenter's Workshop"
Terborch, "The Letter", "Boy ridding his Dog of Fleas"

Italian painters, end of 13th c. to mid 15th c.:
Fra Angelico, "Entombment"
Giotto, "Christ on the Cross"
Filippo Lippi, "Virgin and Child"
Raphael, Canigiani "Holy Family", "Madonna Tenda"
Giorgione, "Portrait of a Man"
Tintoretto, Gonzaga cycle from Mantua

Mathias Grünewald, "SS. Erasmus and Maurice" ▶

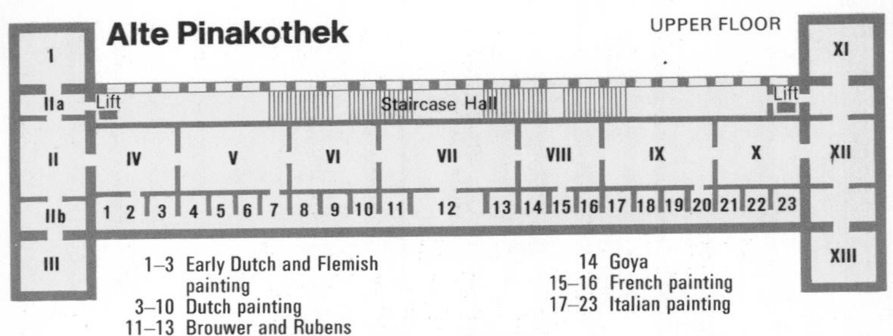

I Altdorfer
II Dürer
IIa Baldung, Cranach
IIb Dürer, Altdorfer
III Cranach, Grünewald
IV Early Dutch and Flemish painters
V Rembrandt
VI Rubens
VII Rubens
VIII Van Dyck
IX Tiepolo, Italian Baroque
X Raphael, Italian Renaissance
XI Spanish painters
XII Titian, Venetians
XIII French painters

Titian, "Emperor Charles V", "The Crowning with Thorns"
Veronese, "Portrait of a Venetian Lady"

Spanish painters of the 16th–18th c.:
El Greco, "Disrobing of Christ", "St Veronica"
Goya, "Plucked Turkey"
Murillo, "Boys eating Melons and Grapes", "Beggar Boys playing with Dice"

French painters of the 15th–18th c.:
Boucher, "Girl resting"
Claude Lorrain, "Banishment of Hagar and Ishmael", "Hagar and Ishmael in the Wilderness"
Poussin, "Lamentation"

*Alter Hof (Old Court) O18

Location
Hofgraben

U-Bahn
Marienplatz

S-Bahn
Marienplatz

The Alter Hof, formerly also known as the Ludwigsburg, was the first residence of the Wittelsbach family in Munich (1253–1474). Built by Duke Ludwig II after the division of Bavaria (1255), its most brilliant period was in the reign of Emperor Ludwig the Bavarian, who ruled the Holy Roman Empire from here in 1328–47. When, at the end of the 14th c., the building proved too small, antiquated and unsafe the Dukes began to build a new fortified residence (see Residence). From the 17th c. the Alter Hof was used only for administrative purposes; it is now occupied by a tax office.

The handsome inner courtyard is open to the public, but not the interior. The four ranges of buildings surrounding the courtyard were much altered and enlarged in later centuries. At the beginning of the 19th c. St Lawrence's Chapel in the north wing and the gate-tower at the south end were pulled down (though the tower was later rebuilt in its original form).

After the Second World War the whole building was restored. The lozenge pattern painted on the walls of the courtyard dates from the 15th c.; it was renewed in the 1960s, following the uncovering of fragments of the original decoration in 1963.

South tower and oriel (the Monkey's Tower) of the Alter Hof

A feature of particular interest is the beautiful Late Gothic oriel in the courtyard, known as the Affenturm (Monkey's Tower). Legend has it that a monkey from the Royal Menagerie carried the infant Prince Ludwig, later the Emperor Ludwig the Bavarian (1314–47), out of his nursery and on to the pointed roof of the oriel, bringing him safely back only after much coaxing.

Amalienpassage

M18

The Amalienpassage cuts through a block to the rear of the University, between Amalienstrasse and Türkenstrasse. It was constructed in 1975–77 by a group of architects following a new concept of urban planning: a grey and unattractive area to the rear of the street frontages was to be opened up, replanned and redeveloped for housing. Although at first the demolition of older property and its replacement by new building at high density met with some resistance, the Amalienpassage is now widely accepted as a successful example of the rehabilitation of the old city centre and has become a popular place of resort for the people of Munich, with shops, cafés and restaurants bringing animation to its three linked courts.

Location
Amalienstrasse 87–89,
Türkenstrasse 84–88

U-Bahn
Universität

*Ammersee

The Ammersee lies amid wooded morainic hills in a basin formed by an Ice Age glacier. It is 16 km (10 miles) long, with

S-Bahn
Herrsching

Distance
39 km (24 miles) SW on B 12 (or Lindau motorway, Argelsried exit)

an average width of 3 km (2 miles), an area of 47 sq. km (18 sq. miles) and a maximum depth of 87 m (285 ft). At the northern and southern ends are areas of bog formed by river flooding. There is a pleasant steamer trip on the lake, calling in at the old villages on its shores (Aidenried, Diessen, St Alban, Riederau, Holzhausen, Utting, Schondorf, Stegen, Buch and Brietbrunn). The lake offers unlimited scope for bathing and water-sports.

Herrsching

This little town of 8000 inhabitants lies in the only inlet on the shores of the lake, the Herrschinger Winkel. From here a road runs south through the Kiental to Andechs Abbey (see entry).

Diessen

This holiday resort (pop. 7500) on the west side of the lake was founded in 1230 by the Count of Andechs. The church of the former Augustinian Monastery (now a girls' boarding-school) was designed by the Rococo architect Johann Michael Fischer, and leading Bavarian artists contributed to its furnishing and decoration. The most notable features are the High Altar (Cuvilliés), the figures of the four Fathers of the Church (Joachim Dietrich), the altar-piece (B. A. Albrecht) and a picture by Tiepolo on the Altar of St Sebastian. The church is in grave danger of collapse.

Andechs Abbey (Kloster Andechs)

S-Bahn
Herrsching

Bus
951

Distance
42 km (26 miles) SW

According to the legend St Rasso (d. 954), a Count of Andechs, brought back from a pilgrimage to Jerusalem three sacred relics, which he preserved on the "sacred mountain" of Andechs (711 m (2333 ft)). When skeletons were found there in the late Middle Ages Andechs developed into a popular place of pilgrimage.

The church of this Benedictine house is a Gothic hall-church with a Rococo interior of 1751–55. The stucco decoration and frescoes were the work of Johann Baptist Zimmermann; the carving on the altars was by Johann Baptist Straub. The sacred image on the High Altar dates from about 1500. The sacristy contains gold reliquaries of the 15th and 16th c. which can be seen by arrangement.

From the tower of the church there are beautiful views of the surrounding area and the hills to the south.

Andechs is also famous for its monastic brewery, where the excellent beer has made the former place of pilgrimage a popular destination at week-ends and at holiday times.

Angel of Peace (Friedensengel) N19/20

Location
Prinzregentenstrasse

Buses
53, 55

The Angel of Peace, prominently situated on the higher east bank of the Isar, was erected by the city of Munich in 1895–99 to commemorate the 25th anniversary of the Peace of Versailles (which ended the Franco-Prussian War of 1870–71) and to honour the Bavarian Army. The gilded figure of the angel (restored 1981–83), modelled on the Nike (Victory) of Olympia, stands on a 23 m (75 ft) high column, the substructure of which is in the form of an open temple portico. From the monument a double staircase descends to the Prinzregentenbrücke.

Angel of Peace

Anthropological Collection

See State Anthropological Collection

*Antiquities, State Collection of

See State Collection of Antiquities

Applied Art, State Museum of

See New Collection

Archbishop's Palace (Erzbischöfliches Palais) N18

The Archbishop's Palace is the principal sight and landmark in Kardinal-Faulhaber-Strasse, a narrow but very busy street which runs between Promenadeplatz and Salvatorstrasse.
This Baroque palace was built by Cuvilliés the Elder in 1733–37 for Countess Holnstein, mistress of Elector Charles Albert. It has a beautifully articulated façade, with a central balcony over the doorway, arched windows protected by grilles and round windows on the ground floor. The stucco ornament (ascribed to J. B. Zimmermann) is less noteworthy than the Early Rococo architecture of the façade.

Location
Kardinal-Faulhaber-Strasse 7

U-Bahn
Odeonsplatz

S-Bahn
Marienplatz

The ruined Bavarian Army Museum

Army Museum (Armeemuseum) N18

Location
Karl-Scharnagl-Ring

U-Bahn
Odeonsplatz

S-Bahn
Isartor

The ruins of the former Army Museum, an imposing domed structure of the Gründerzeit (the period of rapid industrial expansion in the early 1870s), stand at the east end of the Hofgarten (see entry). The building is in grave danger of collapse, and for many years was on the point of being pulled down, until in the early 1970s its importance in the townscape of Munich was recognised. Since then there has been much discussion of its restoration and possible future use.

Artists' House

See Künstlerhaus

**Asam Church (Asamkirche) O17

Location
Sendlinger Strasse 62

U-Bahn
Sendlinger-Tor-Platz

S-Bahn
Marienplatz

This beautiful Rococo church, dedicated to St John of Nepomuk, was built between 1733 and 1746 by the brothers Cosmas Damian and Egid Quirin Asam and richly decorated with stucco ornament, stucco figures, frescoes and oil-paintings.
The church's narrow façade fits unobtrusively into the line of buildings on Sendlinger Strasse. The doorway is flanked by

The richly decorated Rococo interior of the Asam Church ▶

massive columns, and above it is a figure of St John of Nepomuk kneeling in prayer.
In the interior of the church a wrought-iron grille (1776) separates the oval vestibule, with carved confessionals and stucco figures of saints, from the long nave with its galeries and projecting cornice under the ceiling. On the ceiling is a magnificent fresco on the life of St John of Nepomuk by C. D. Asam (restored 1977).
The impressive twilight effect of the interior is created by its concealed windows. When, during restoration work in the 1970s, a large window was inserted in the choir and the church was flooded with light there was a bitter controversy among art historians about the authenticity of this change, and in the end the authorities responsible for the conservation of historical monuments decided that the window must be closed up.
The most notable feature of the interior is the High Altar, enclosed by four twisted columns. On the altar is a glass shrine containing a wax figure of St John of Nepomuk. The altar in the gallery depicts the Trinity, with two angels in adoration. On the cornice above the High Altar is God the Father, in a Papal tiara, bending over the Crucified Christ, with the dove representing the Holy Ghost in an aureole above.

*Asam House (Asamhaus) O17

Location
Sendlinger Strasse 61

U-Bahn
Sendlinger-Tor-Platz

S-Bahn
Marienplatz

This 16th c. house was acquired in 1733 by Egid Quirin Asam, who decorated it with lavish stucco ornament, giving plastic form to the South German technique of *Lüftelmalerei* (painted decoration on the external walls of houses). The themes of the decoration are man's artistic activity and the sensuous world (lower half), and heaven as conceived by Christianity and by classical antiquity (upper half).

Auer Dult P18/19

Location
Mariahilfplatz (Au)

Bus
52

Trams
15, 25, 27

The Dult is a traditional fair held three times a year in the square in front of the Mariahilfkirche in the Au district – in May (the May Fair), July (St James's Fair) and October (the church's patronal festival). In addition to roundabouts, swings, shooting galleries, sideshows, a Punch and Judy show and a giant wheel the attractions include a huge market selling kitchenware, porcelain, antiques and junk of all kinds – everything from commonplace domestic equipment to old books and peasant-style furniture.

*Bavaria Figure and Hall of Fame (Bavaria, Ruhmeshalle) P16

Location
Theresienhöhe 16

U-Bahn
Goetheplatz

S-Bahn
Hackerbrücke

The colossal figure of Bavaria, representing a woman in the old German style, was modelled by Lugwig Schwanthaler and cast in bronze by Ferdinand von Miller in 1844–50. Weighing 792 kilograms (1560 cwt), it was the largest bronze figure ever cast. Bavaria is clad in a long garment and a bearskin; in her raised left hand she holds a garland of oak leaves, in her right hand a sword. Beside her sits a lion, the heraldic animal of Bavaria. A

Stalls at the Auer Dult

Bavaria and the Hall of Fame

Trams
14, 27

Opening times
Interior: Tue.–Sun.
10 a.m.–midday and
2–5.30 p.m.

flight of 126 steps leads up inside the statue to the head, from which there is an extensive view over the city.
To the rear of the statue is the Hall of Fame (Ruhmeshalle), an open Doric portico built by Leo von Klenze in 1843–53. It contains 80 busts of notable Bavarian figures, some of them badly damaged.

**Bavarian National Museum (Bayerisches Nationalmuseum) N19

Location
Prinzregentenstrasse 3

Tram
20

Buses
53, 55

Opening times
Apr.–Sep., Tue.–Fri.
9.30 a.m.–4.30 p.m., Sat., Sun. and pub. hol. 10 a.m.–4.30 p.m.; Oct.–Mar., Tue.–Fri. 9 a.m.–4 p.m., Sat., Sun. and pub. hol. 9.30 a.m.–4 p.m.

The Bavarian National Museum consists of two sections, one devoted to art and applied art, the other to folk art and traditions. The former displays South German sculpture, painting and applied arts from the Middle Ages to the 19th c., with special collections of clocks and watches, glass, porcelain, faience, miniatures, ivories and goldsmith's work. The folk section includes rooms from peasant houses, pottery, traditional costumes, peasant implements and utensils, and a celebrated collection of cribs (Nativity groups).
The straggling range of buildings which houses the National Museum dates from the heyday of the "historical" style. Its architect was Gabriel von Seidl, who designed each section of the building in a different style: the main block Baroque, the east wing Romanesque, the west wing Renaissance, the projecting wings on the street side Late Baroque to Rococo. The upper floor at the east end occupied by the National Prehistoric Collection (see entry) was added in 1937 (architect German Bestelmeyer).
Particularly notable exhibits:
Romanesque statuary in wood and stone (Room 1)
Woodcarving by Tilmann Riemenschneider (Room 16) and Hans Leinberger (Room 21), dating from about 1500
South German bronzes by Hans Krumper and Hubert Gerhard, of about 1600 (Rooms 19 and 30)
18th c. sculpture in wood by Ignaz Günther and Johann Baptist Straub (Rooms 42 and 43)

*Blutenburg Castle (Schloss Blutenburg) L9

Location
S of Verdistrasse

S-Bahn
Obermenzing

Buses
73, 75, 76

Opening times
Daily 2–5 p.m.

Blutenburg Castle was built by Duke Albert II in 1438–39 as a hunting-lodge, replacing an older castle which had been burned down in war. It was defended by a ring wall, towers and a moat. After being destroyed during the Thirty Years War it was rebuilt in 1680–81 as a plain rectangular structure.
The castle now houses the International Youth Library, a collection of literature for children and young people in 110 languages, at present totalling some 400,000 volumes.
A unique jewel of Late Gothic architecture, both the building and its furnishings being preserved in their original form, is the castle's chapel (1488), dedicated to St Sigismund. The fragments of frescoes on the exterior walls give some idea of what the external painting (now lost) of Munich's Late Gothic churches was like.
Features of particular interest: altar-pieces by Jan Polack (*c.* 1490); paintings on High Altar (Christ as Judge and Baptism, to right; Coronation of Virgin, to left); wooden figures of the Twelve Apostles and the famous Blutenburg Madonna

Bavarian National Museum

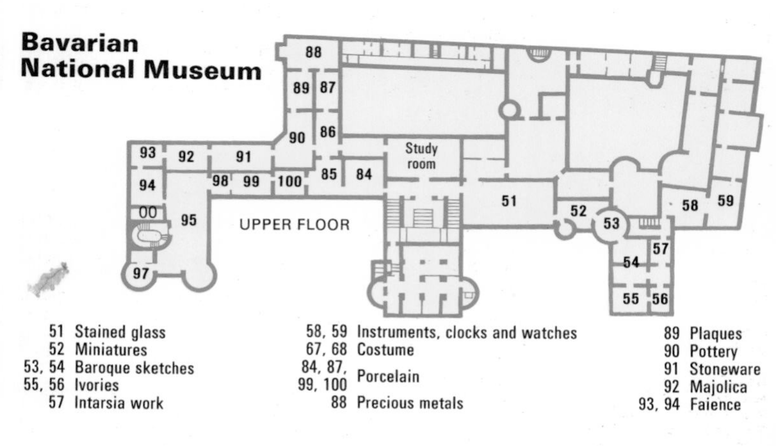

51 Stained glass
52 Miniatures
53, 54 Baroque sketches
55, 56 Ivories
57 Intarsia work
58, 59 Instruments, clocks and watches
67, 68 Costume
84, 87, 99, 100 Porcelain
88 Precious metals
89 Plaques
90 Pottery
91 Stoneware
92 Majolica
93, 94 Faience

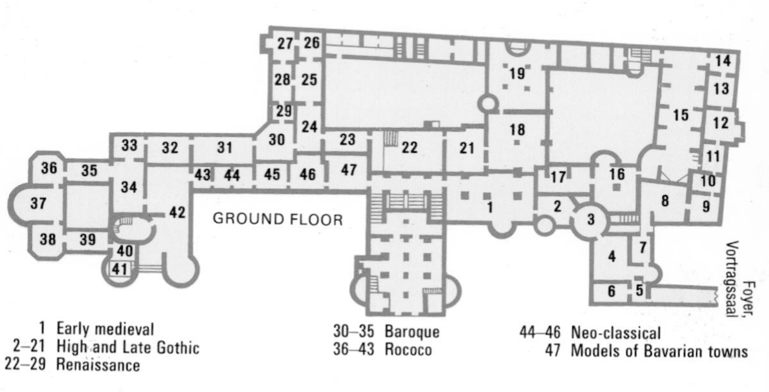

1 Early medieval
2–21 High and Late Gothic
22–29 Renaissance
30–35 Baroque
36–43 Rococo
44–46 Neo-classical
47 Models of Bavarian towns

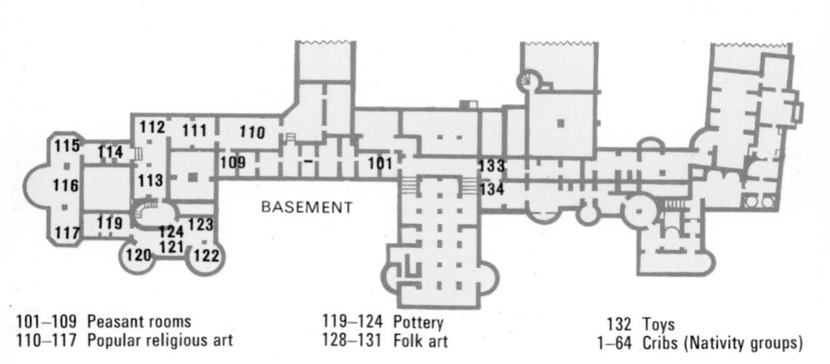

101–109 Peasant rooms
110–117 Popular religious art
119–124 Pottery
128–131 Folk art
132 Toys
1–64 Cribs (Nativity groups)

Blutenburg: courtyard and chapel

(beside tabernacle) by the unidentified Master of the Blutenburg Madonna; stained glass (16 scenes, from Annunciation to Passion; Wittelsbach coats of arms) by Martin the Glazier.

BMW Museum

J17

Location
Petuelring 130

U-Bahn
Petuelring, Olympiazentrum

Buses
36, 41, 43, 81, 84, 136, 184

Opening times
Daily 9 a.m.–5 p.m.

The BMW Museum, adjoining Munich's new landmark, the cloverleaf-shaped offices of the Bayerische Motorwerke (Bavarian Motor Works: hence BMW), displays a collection of BMW cars, motor-cycles and engines. Almost all the vehicles produced by this old-established automobile firm are represented, from the Dixi which was popular in the 1920s to the showy sports and racing models of the 1950s and 1960s, from the R 32 motor cycle of 1932 to the world record winner of 1955. The museum was remodelled at great cost in 1980 by the multimedia artist Eberhard Schoener and the theatrical designer Wilfried Minks.

Bonifatiusbasilika

See St Boniface's Church

*Botanic Gardens (Botanischer Garten) L12

The present Botanic Gardens on the north side of Nymphenburg Park were laid out between 1909 and 1914, the previous gardens near the Karlsplatz having suffered ill effects from environmental influences. The wide range of plants grown here and the well-designed landscaping rank the Munich Botanic Gardens among the finest of their kind in Europe.
Features of the gardens are a large arboretum with both deciduous and coniferous trees, an Alpine garden with rocks and plants from the Alps, a fern gorge and a rhododendron grove, and sections devoted to medicinal and industrial plants, protected species, genetics and ecology. Exotic plants grown in the greenhouses include orchids (for which the gardens are famous), cacti and insectivorous plants.

Location
Nymphenburg,
Menzinger Strasse 63

Trams
17, 21

Opening times
Daily 9 a.m.–7 p.m., winter to 4.30 p.m. Greenhouses 9–11.45 a.m. and 1–6.30 p.m., winter to 4 p.m.

Brienner Strasse N17/18

This handsome street was laid out at the beginning of the 19th c., in the reign of King Maximilian I, during the development of the Maxvorstadt. While that district is laid out on a strictly rectangular plan the Brienner Strasse is opened up by a series of magnificent squares (Wittelsbacher Platz (see entry), Karolinenplatz (see entry), Königsplatz (see entry)). The layout was designed by Karl von Fischer and continued after his death by Leo von Klenze.
The houses in the street, originally in Empire, neo-Renaissance

U-Bahn
Odeonsplatz, Königsplatz

S-Bahn
Marienplatz, Königsplatz

Alpine garden in the Botanic Gardens

and neo-classical styles, were occupied by aristocratic families, leading citizens and prominent artists. The original structure of the street has suffered much damage from wartime destruction, the alteration of the older buildings and the construction of office buildings for banks and insurance companies.
In the Platz der Opfer des Nationalsozialismus (Square of the Victims of National Socialism) the busy Altstadtring (the ring of wide boulevards surrounding the old town) crosses the Brienner Strasse, destroying the original unity of its conception.

* Bürgersaal — O17

Location
Neuhauser Strasse 48

U-Bahn
Marienplatz

S-Bahn
Karlsplatz

This Citizens' hall, the meeting-place and place of worship of the Marian Congregation (a community under Jesuit direction), was built in 1709–10 to the design of Giovanni Antonio Viscardi and has been used as a church since 1778. It was destroyed during the Second World War and rebuilt in 1945–46.
The façade with its double pilasters is still in its original condition apart from the side doors, which were later insertions. In a niche over the main doorway is a figure of the Virgin and Child on a crescent moon.
On the lower floor is the Tomb of Rupert Mayer (1876–1945), a Jesuit who worked for the Resistance against the Nazi régime. On the upper floor is the restored Baroque prayer hall, notable features of which are the Guardian Angel group (by Ignaz Günther, 1763) under the organ gallery and a landscape-painting by F. J. Beich (1710) depicting old Marian places of pilgrimage in Bavaria.

Church of the Assumption (Mariä Himmelfahrt) — S16

Location
Fraunbergplatz 1,
Thalkirchen

Buses
31, 57

Of the original Late Romanesque church (second half of 13th c.) there remain only parts of the tower and the choir wall. The present church was built about 1400, remodelled in Baroque style in 1692 and enlarged by an extension at the west end in 1907–08 (architect G. von Seidl).
The Baroque altars and pulpit date from about 1700; the image of the Virgin and the figures of bishops on the High Altar are ascribed to M. Erhard (1492). About 1760 Ignaz Günther again altered the High Altar, adding the figures of SS. Joachim and Anne and the angels.

Coin Collection

See State Coin Collection

** Cuvilliés Theatre (Cuvilliéstheater) — N18

Location
Residenzstrasse 1
(entrance in Brunnenhof)

The Cuvilliés Theatre, officially known as the Old Residence Theatre (Altes Residenztheater), is the finest Rococo theatre with tiers of boxes in Germany.
Built by François Cuvilliés in 1750–55, it was destroyed during

The sumptuous Rococo interior of the Cuvilliés Theatre

the Second World War but was rebuilt in its original form in 1956–58 with the magnificent carved woodwork which had been stored in a place of safety during the war.

The first performance of Mozart's "Idomeneo" was given in this theatre in 1781, and it is still used for operatic and dramatic performances and concerts.

The richly decorated auditorium, in red, white and gold, has a distinctive atmosphere of its own. The tiers of boxes, the Electoral Box and the proscenium boxes are decorated with superb carving (imitations of fabrics, draped curtains, reliefs, garlands). Graceful carved figures appear to perform an architectural function as supports. Among the artist who contributed to the decoration of the theatre were Johann Baptist Straub, Joachim and Michael Dietrich and Johann Baptist Zimmermann, whose frescoes were destroyed by bombing.

Telephone
22 46 41

U-Bahn
Odeonsplatz

S-Bahn
Marienplatz

Opening times
Sun. and pub. hol. 10 a.m.–5 a.m., Mon.–Sat. 2–5 p.m.

Dachau

This little town of 35,000 inhabitants lies north-west of Munich on the steep left bank of the River Amper. First mentioned in 805, the place received its municipal charter only in 1933. The writer Ludwig Thoma (see Noted Personalities) practised as a lawyer in Dachau before moving to Munich. During the Nazi period Dachau became notorious as the site of the Dachau concentration camp (see Dachau Concentration Camp Memorial Site).

The Dachauer Moos (Dachau Moss), an attractive area of bog

S-Bahn
Dachau

Distance
17 km (10½ miles) NW

and pastureland, has largely been drained and brought into cultivation. Its scenery attracted many 19th c. landscape-painters.
Dachau has a Schloss, which is merely one wing, remodelled by Joseph Effner in the 18th c., of a massive 16th c. Renaissance palace, the rest of which has been demolished. The staircase hall and west front (1715) are in French Regency style. The banqueting hall on the upper floor, with a grisaille frieze by Hans Thonauer, is used in August for exhibitions by Dachau painters. Behind the Schloss is a large Baroque garden.

Dachau Concentration Camp Memorial Site (KD-Gedenkstätte)

Location
Alte Römerstrasse

S-Bahn
Dachau

Bus
Municipal bus from Dachau Station

Opening times
Daily 9 a.m.–5 p.m.; documentary film at 11 a.m. and 3 p.m.

The Dachau memorial was erected after the war on the site of the notorious Nazi concentration camp. Of the prisoners confined in the camp, over 200,000 in number – mainly Jews, gipsies, clergymen, Communists and opponents of the régime – some 32,000 lost their lives.
The layout of the hutments occupied by the prisoners can still be identified on the ground. The former workshops and offices now house a museum (photographs, films, documents) illustrating the atrocities committed by the Nazi authorities. In front of the museum is the International Memorial (1968), a stylised representation of prisoners behind barbed wire. At the other end of the site are the expiatory chapels – the Jewish Memorial of Israel (right), the Roman Catholic Chapel of Christ's Agony (centre) and the Protestant Church of Reconciliation (left). At the north-west corner of the camp is the crematorium for the burning and disposal of prisoners' corpses.

**Deutsches Museum

See German Museum

*Dreifaltigkeitskirche

See Trinity Church

Egyptian Collection (Ägyptische Sammlung)

N18

Location
Residence, Hofgartenstrasse 1 (at obelisk)

U-Bahn
Odeonsplatz

S-Bahn
Marienplatz

Bus
55

The State Collection of Egyptian Art is housed on the ground floor of the Residence (see entry), on either side of the passage into the Kaiserhof. One of the oldest museums of its kind, it grew out of the collections assembled by Duke Albert V and King Ludwig I (1825–48). During the 19th c. it acquired much additional material from donations. The present museum also contains the Egyptian antiquities formerly held by the Glyptothek (see entry).
The collection covers the whole range of ancient Egyptian history – the Pre-dynastic period (4500–3000 B.C.), the Period of Unification (about 3000 B.C.), the Old Kingdom (5th and 6th

Egyptian obelisk outside the Residenz

Dynasties, 2660–2160 B.C.), Middle Kingdom (11th–13th Dynasties, 2040–1160 B.C.) and New Kingdom (18th–20th Dynasties, 1550–1080 B.C.), the Late period (25th–30th Dynasties), the Graeco-Roman period (700 B.C. to end of 3rd c. A.D.) and the Coptic Period (4th–9th c. A.D.).

The material on display includes sculpture and reliefs, jewellery and ornaments, cult objects, domestic and other implements, sarcophagi, papyri and textiles.

Items of particular interest include the following:

A limestone statue of a seated female figure from the earliest temple precinct at Abydos (Period of Unification).

A thin-walled goblet of green slate (Period of Unification).

A granite group of Dersenet and his family, false doors from the Tomb of Meni, and slaughtering scenes from the Tomb of Ni-auch-nesent at Sakkara (Old Kingdom).

A copper figure of an unclothed man and a cult image (bronze and gold) of the crocodile god Sobek (Middle Kingdom).

A limestone lion's head, the head of a sphinx (Amenophis II), a squatting figure of a high priest of Amun, and a hoard of weapons from Sichem (New Kingdom).

A bronze figure of Osiris and the gold treasure of Queen Amanisha-heto from her pyramid at Meroe in the Sudan (Late period).

A glass figure of a youth (intarsia work) and painted pottery (Coptic art).

Opening times
Tue.–Sun. 9.30 a.m.–4 p.m.; also 7–9 p.m. Tue.

*Englischer Garten (English Garden) J21–N19

U-Bahn
Universität, Giselastrasse, Münchener Freiheit

The Englischer Garten is the largest and one of the most beautiful city parks in Germany. With its naturally arranged groups of trees and plants, offering ever-changing vistas, its winding streams and its large artificial lake it gives the impression of a mature natural landscape.

In 1785, on the suggestion of Sir Benjamin Thompson (later created Count von Rumford), Elector Charles Theodore laid out on the banks of the Isar a Military Garden which, in his own words, was to "serve not only for the benefit and recreation of the military but also for general use as a public promenade". The landscaping of the garden was the work of Sir Benjamin Thompson, Baron Reinhard von Werneck and Ludwig von Sckell.

In 1789 various schools and model farms and other establishments, providing training in agriculture, forestry, dairy-farming, sheep-farming and horticulture, were set up in the garden. The lake was formed in 1802 under the direction of Reinhard von Werneck; and in 1810–11 the garden was extended and the lake enlarged by Ludwig von Sckell.

The Englischer Garten still serves for "the exercise and social recreation" of the people of Munich and for "the enjoyment of free and healthy air" as its founder intended, and in spring and summer is a popular resort for both old and young, who come here to walk, lounge about, sunbathe, make music, play games, ride, take a boat out and drink beer (beer-gardens at the Chinese Tower and on the lake).

From the Monopteros, a classical-style temple (by Leo von

Englischer Garten: the Monopteros (left) and Chinese Tower (right)

Klenze, 1837–38) on an artificial hill, there is a very fine view of the old part of the town. This was notorious in the 1960s as the haunt of drop-outs.
The Chinese Tower, a pagoda-like structure, was built by J. Frey in 1789–90 as an outlook tower and bandstand. Burned down in 1944, it was rebuilt in 1951.
The building to the south of the Chinese Tower, now housing a café-restaurant, and the Rumfordhaus (135 metres (150 yd) north), a former officers' mess, were erected in 1790 (architect J. B. Lechner).
The Seehaus (Lake House) on the shores of the lake, built by Gabriel von Seidl in 1883, was demolishd in 1970, having fallen into a state of dilapidation, and has been replaced by a new building.
The handsome Aujägermeisterhaus (Huntsman's House) at the north end of the Englischer Garten was built in 1810–11 (architect Deiglmayr).

Ethnology, State Museum of

See State Museum of Ethnology

European Patent Office (Europäisches Patentamt) P18

In the early 1970s the Municipal Council authorised the demolition of older houses in Ehrhardtstrasse and the construction of a high-rise office block to house the European Patent Office – a project which had encountered much opposition from local people. Within a few years the huge reinforced-concrete structure had been completed, and in 1980 the European Patent Office moved in. It now employs a staff of several thousand.
Since the 1970s there has been much building activity in the adjoining area along the banks of the Isar.

Location
Ehrhardtstrasse

S-Bahn
Isartor

Trams
19, 20

Buses
52, 56

Feldherrnhalle (Commanders' Hall) N18

The Feldherrnhalle, an open loggia (by Friedrich von Gärtner, 1841–44; 20 m (66 ft high)) modelled on the Loggia dei Lanzi in Florence, closes the vista at the south end of Ludwigstrasse. It contains bronze figures (by Ludwig Schwanthaler) of two great Bavarian commanders, General Tilly (1559–1632) General and Wrede (1767–1838), honoured here by desire of King Ludwig I. The Bavarian Army Memorial commemorates the Franco-Prussian War of 1870–71. The two lions on the steps were the work of W. Ruemann (1905); one is popularly said to be growling at the Residence, the other to be keeping its mouth shut towards the church.

Location
Odeonsplatz

U-Bahn
Odeonsplatz

Food Market

See Viktualienmarkt

Frauenkirche

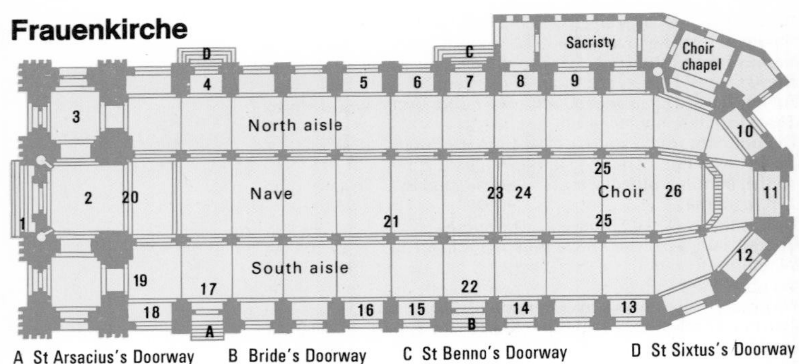

A St Arsacius's Doorway B Bride's Doorway C St Benno's Doorway D St Sixtus's Doorway

1 Entrance to tower
2 St Christopher (1520)
3 Mariahilf Altar (*c.* 1473)
4 St George (16th c.)
5 Tomb of the first priest (1502)
6 Ecce Homo (1640)
7 St Sebastian (18th c.)
8 Assumption (1620)
9 St Pius's Chapel
10 Baptism (*c.* 1510)
11 Virgin of Mercy (*c.* 1510)
12 Crucifixion (*c.* 1450)
13 Ligsalcz gravestone (1300)
14 Baptistery
15 Three Kings (*c.* 1650)
16 Patron of bakers (16th c.)
17 St Rasso (15th c.)
18 Tomb of J. M. Fischer (d. 1766)
19 Tomb of Ludwig the Bavarian (1622)
20 Great Organ (1959)
21 Pulpit (1959)
22 St Andrew's Organ (1959)
23 Cross (1951)
24 Altar
25 Figures by Erasmus Grasser (1502)
26 Bishop's throne

** Frauenkirche (Church of Our Lady) O18

Location
Frauenplatz

U-Bahn
Marienplatz

S-Bahn
Marienplatz, Karlsplatz

Opening times
South tower: spring and Oct., 9 a.m.–6 p.m.; summer 8.30 a.m.–7 p.m.

The Frauenkirche has been the cathedral and metropolitan church of the South Bavarian ecclesiastical provinces since the establishment of the archbishopric of Munich and Freising in 1821.

This brick-built Late Gothic church owes its impact to its great size (109 m (358 ft) by 40 m (131 ft)), its high walls, its clear articulation and its lack of ornament. With its sturdy twin towers, rearing up to a height of 99 m (325 ft) and 100 m (328 ft), it is Munich's most celebrated landmark.

The Frauenkirche was built in 1468–88 by Jörg Halspach (known as Ganghofer) on the site of an earlier chapel dedicated to the Virgin. In place of the spires originally planned by Halspach the two towers were given their characteristic Renaissance domes in 1525; the green patina of the domes harmonises well with the dark red brick. The carved medallions on the five doorways were the work of Ignaz Günther (1772). – The church suffered severe damage in 1944–45. Restoration work was completed in 1953.

Interior

The interior of this aisled hall-church, with 22 tall octagonal pillars in two rows, was remodelled in Renaissance style in 1601 but reconverted to a Gothic design in 1858. As rebuilt after its destruction in the last war it has a simply conceived but very effective whitewashed interior.

The aisles and windows cannot be seen from the porch, since the octagonal pillars of the nave have the appearance of a wall. The window of the choir was formerly concealed by the High Altar. (Legend has it that the Devil came to inspect the church after its completion and was so delighted that the windows had been forgotten that he stamped his foot, leaving a footprint in the porch that can still be seen.)

In going round the church the following features should not be missed:

An over-life-size figure of St Christopher in wood (*c.* 1515).

The Cross by Josef Heuselmann (1954).

Figures of the Apostles and Prophets from the former choir-stalls, carved by Erasmus Grasser (1502).

A figure of St Sebastian by Andreas Faistenberger (18th c.).

An altar-piece of the Assumption by Peter Candid (1620), formerly on the High Altar.

Twelve reliefs by Ignaz Günther in the Schutzmantelkapelle (Chapel of the Virgin of Mercy).

A figure of St George attributed to Hans Leinberger (*c.* 1520).

A bronze relief of the Raising of Lazarus (1596) by Hubert Gerhard in the Bäckerkapelle (Bakers' Chapel).

Particularly notable is the tomb of the Emperor Ludwig the Bavarian, a free-standing monument of black marble with magnificent bronze figures. It was designed by Hans Krumper, who was also responsible for the bronze figures of William IV and Albert V; the armour-clad standard-bearers at the four corners were the work of Hubert Gerhard (1595). Not easily visible is the red marble slab (Late Gothic, attributed to Erasmus Grasser) from the original tomb, which depicts the Emperor enthroned and Albert III's reconciliation with his father after their disagreement over his marriage to Agnes Bernauer.

The stained glass in the choir is 14th c.; that in the aisles is modern.

In the crypt are the tombs of bishops of Munich and Freising (including Cardinals Faulhaber, Wendel and Döpfner).

The twin towers of the Frauenkirche

* Freising Cathedral (Dom zu Freising)

Location
Domberg

S-Bahn
Freising

Distance
33 km (20½ miles) N

The town Freising (pop. 35,000), on the left bank of the Isar, was founded in 739 by St Boniface as the see of a bishop and became a major centre for the propagation of Christianity in Bavaria. In 1803 the bishopric was secularised; then in 1821 it became part of the archbishopric of Munich and Freising, with the archbishop's seat in Munich.

Freising Cathedral, a five-aisled Romanesque basilica, was built between 1160 and 1205, given its vaulted roof in 1480–82 and lavishly decorated by the Asam brothers in 1723–24 with stucco ornament and paintings. Since 1983 it has had the status of a Co-Cathedral.

From the Gothic porch between the twin towers a stepped Romanesque doorway (figures of Emperor Frederick Barbarossa, Bishop Albert I, Empress Beatrice) leads into the interior. The principal feature of the church is the large Romanesque crypt (1160), which has survived in its original form. Among the 24 columns, in three rows, which support the vaulting, with capitals of varying form, is a famous "animal column", made up of the intertwined bodies of men and monsters.

The 15th c. cloister on the east side of the church was decorated with frescoes and stucco-work by Johann Baptist Zimmermann in 1716. On its east side is a Benedictine church of 1345 with stucco-work of 1716.

The Diocesan Museum at Domberg 21 (open Tue.–Fri. 10 a.m.–4 p.m., Sat. and Sun. 10 a.m.–6 p.m. pub. hol. 10 a.m.–4 p.m.) contains works of sacred art, pictures and maps illustrating the history of the bishopric of Freising.

Fürstenfeldbruck Monastery (Kloster Fürstenfeldbruck)

S-Bahn
Fürstenfeldbruck

Distance
23 km (14 miles) W

In 1256 Duke Ludwig the Severe, suspecting his wife Maria of Brabant of infidelity, caused her to be executed; but, when it was later established that she had not been unfaithful to him, he was required by the Pope to found a monastery in atonement for his offence.

In 1263 the monastery moved to its present site on the Fürstenfeld (Prince's Field) near the little town of Bruck, and became the private monastery and burial-place of the Wittelsbach dynasty.

The present monastery was built by Giovanni Antonio Viscardi between 1692 and 1704. The spendid Baroque church, also designed by him, was built later (1718–36). Its imposing façade is a characteristic example of the monumental style of Late Baroque façades in southern Germany. The interior is sumptuously decorated with frescoes and stucco-work by the Asam brothers (nave) and Francesco Appiani (choir).

Fürstenried Castle (Schloss Fürstenried)

Location
Forst-Kasten-Allee, Fürstenried

This hunting-lodge was built by Joseph Effner in 1715–17 for Elector Max Emanuel. From 1886 to 1916 it was the residence of King Otto of Bavaria, who was insane. Since 1925 it has

Fürstenfeldbruck Monastery: the Baroque façade and interior of the church

been a house of retreat belonging to the archbishopric of Munich and Freising.
The castle if strictly symmetrical in plan, with three cube-shaped blocks linked by galleries. The avenue of lime-trees in front of the castle is directly aligned on the towers of the Frauenkirche which can be seen in the distance.

Buses
34, 61, 66

Tram
16

Gärtnerplatz Theatre (Gärtnerplatztheater) P18

The Gärtnerplatz Theatre is, after the National Theatre (see entry), Munich's second opera house (opera, ballet), and is also the only theatre in the city which puts on classical operattas and modern musicals.
The architecture and decoration of the theatre, designed by Franz Michael Reifenstuel and built in 1864–65, are in late neo-classical style. The loss of the rich interior decoration as a result of renovation in 1937, together with the removal of the cornices, gables, round-arched windows and other decorative features of the exterior, reduced this once splendid "Temple of the Muses" to a shadow of its former self. Since the restoration of the interior in 1968–69 and the sumptuous original façade in 1980–81, however, the theatre has recovered its former magnificence.

Location
Gärtnerplatz 3

U-Bahn
Fraunhoferstrasse

Buses
52, 56

Trams
18, 20

Gasteig Cultural Centre (Gasteig-Kulturzentrum) O/P19

Location
Am Gasteig

S-Bahn
Isartor, Rosenheimer Platz

Tram
18

Gasteig is the name of an area of higher ground on the east bank of the Isar where a huge new cultural centre has been under construction since 1979 on the site of the old Bürgerbräukeller (a beer-house). In addition to a large modern concert hall with seating for 2400 which will relieve the pressure on the city's over-taxed concert halls, the complex includes accommodation for a variety of cultural institutions – the Richard Strauss Conservatoire, the Volkshochschule (adult education centre), the Central Library and the Municipal Libraries Department, the Department of Culture and the Munich Philharmonic Orchestra.

The project has become notorious for its enormous and steadily increasing cost. In 1980 the municipal authorities announced that the original estimated cost of 162 million DM would be much more than doubled by the time the centre was completed.

**German Museum (Deutsches Museum) P18/19

Location
Museumsinsel

S-Bahn
Isartor

Opening times
Daily 9 a.m.–5 p.m.

Conducted tours
By arrangement

The "German Museum for Master-Works of Science and Technology" is the world's largest museum of technology, covering an area of 40,000 sq. m (48,000 sq. yd) and displaying some 15,000 exhibits. The collections are constantly being expanded by the addition of the latest technological developments.

The museum was founded in 1903 and directed in its early years by Oskar von Miller. Since 1925 it has been housed in a large complex built by Gabriel von Seidl on an island in the Isar, later supplemented by a library, a conference hall and a hall for motor vehicles.

The various departments are excellently arranged, with clear explanations which enable visitors to follow the development of each particular scientific discipline and field of technology. The methods of presentation include scientific apparatus, demonstrations of experiments, machines and machinery, models and picture displays.

The Library of the German Museum, a reference library in the fields of science and technology, has some 650,000 volumes, 1900 periodicals and collections of technical journals, plans, patents, catalogues, manuscipts and other documents.

The Conference Hall on the north side of the museum complex is the largest hall in Munich, with seating for 2400. It is used for concerts and other cultural events as well as for conferences and congresses.

The following is a selection of some exhibits of particular interest:

Basement

Iron-, salt- and coal-mines, with accurate reproductions of the various techniques – shaft-drilling, transport underground, lighting, ventilation, control of water – in 19th c. pits; examples of 20th c. machinery for the working and transport of minerals. Processing, coke and briquette production.

Ground floor

Iron and steel production.
Metalworking: forging, rolling, drawing, casting, welding, cutting, soldering, testing of materials, machine tools.

German Museum

BASEMENT
1 Mining
2 Processing of iron, coal and salt
3 Steam-boilers
4 Shipping
5 Hydraulic engineering
6 Motor vehicles

GROUND FLOOR
7 Iron and steel
8 Oil, natural gas, protection of the environment
9 Opencast mining
10 Minerals
11 V2 rockets
12 Road- and bridge-building
13 Canals, ports, hydraulic engineering
14 Power generation and distribution
15 Shipping
16 Motor vehicles
17 Machine tools
18 Metalworking
19 Air travel and space travel (in course of development)
20 Tunnel construction
21 Model railway
22 Mountain railways
23 Land transport

FIRST FLOOR
24 Nuclear energy
25 Picture Room
26 Chemical engineering
27 Chemistry
 a Pharmacy
 b Laboratories
 c Alchemy
28 Aeronautics
29 Physics
 a Mechanics
 b Electricity
 c Optics
 d Geodesy
30 Atomic and nuclear physics
31 Musical instruments
32 Communications technology

SECOND FLOOR
33 Ceramics
34 Glass
35 Paper-making, bookbinding
36 Writing and printing
37 Photography
38 Textile technology
39 Early crafts

THIRD FLOOR
Space travel
Agricultural technology (including dairying, milling, distilling, brewing)
Weights and measures
The measurement of time
Observatory (up to fourth floor)

FIFTH FLOOR
Astronomy

SIXTH FLOOR
Planetarium

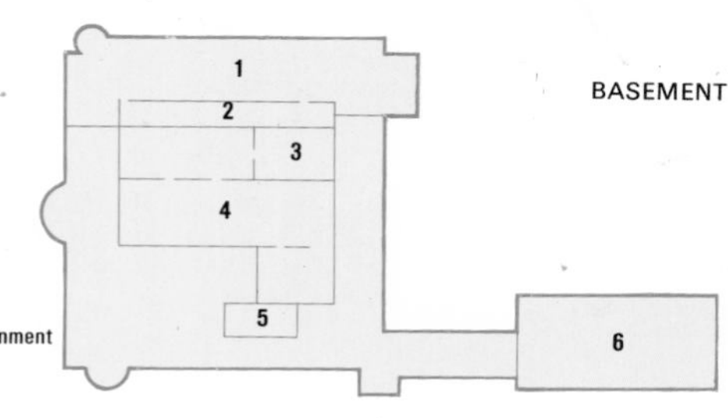

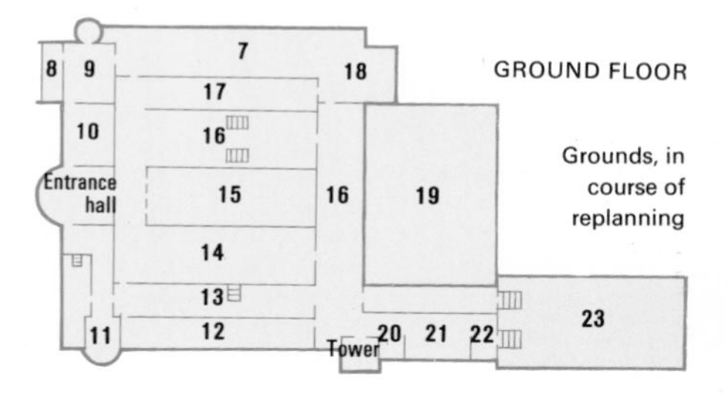

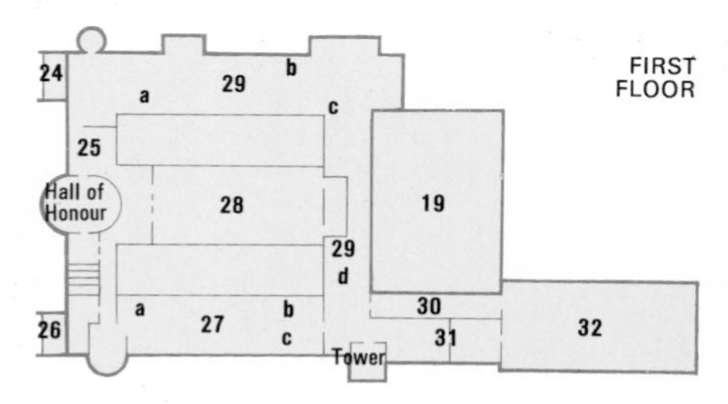

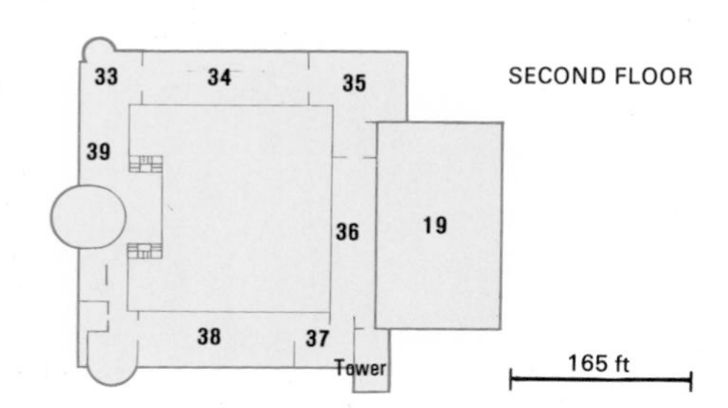

Powered machinery: steam-boilers and steam-engines (oldest steam-engine in Germany, 1813; Watt's steam-engine, 1788; steam turbines, *c.* 1885; water-driven turbines, internal-combustion engines; first diesel engine, 1897; first Daimler automobile engines, 1885 onwards; first Wankel engines, 1957–58).
Power technology: historical development of electric motors (19th c.); functioning of DC and AC motors (experimental demonstrations); three-phase current technology; high-tension system.
Hydraulic engineering: river regulation, canal construction, weirs, hydroelectric power stations, locks, hoists; coastal protection, land reclamation; harbours, inland and marine; navigational aids.
Land transport: sleighs, coaches (Ludwig II's state coach, 1878), bicycles, motor cycles (Megola, 1922; BMW and NSU world-record-winning machines), railways ("Puffing Billy", 1813; first Siemens electric locomotive, 1879); development of the wheel.
Motor vehicles: goods vehicles, utility vehicles (Volkswagen amphibious vehicle, 1944), automobiles (Bugatti, 1926; Mercedes, 1922–23; Lancia Lambda, 1923; Auto Union racing car, 1936–37; Mercedes racing car, 1938–39; Mercedes 300 SLR, 1955; Porsche 917, 1971).
Road and bridge construction: development of roads (section of a Germanic plank roadway, 700 B.C.); timber, stone, steel and concrete bridges.
Shipping: development of the ship, illustrated by models; sailing-ship of 1800; "U1", the first German submarine (original, 1906); technical details, machinery, weapons (torpedoes, mines).
Tunnelling: rock-drilling machines, sections of tunnels (Simplon Tunnel, Munich Underground tunnel).

In the German Museum

Grounds

The grounds of the museum are not open to the public during the construction of a new aero-space hall. The only item at present in the grounds is a Dutch windmill of 1866.

First floor

Physics: nuclear energy, with demonstrations room (opened 1977); mechanics; electricity and magnetism; optics; nuclear physics; nuclear technology.
Aeronautics: development of flying, illustrated by pictures and models; the balloon, the airship, the parachute, the kite, gliding, powered flight (piston engine, gas turbines, jet engines, airscrews, rockets).
Aircraft (originals): Lilienthal, 1895; Wright, 1909; Grade, 1909; Blériot, 1909; Etrich-Rumpler Taube, 1910; Fokker fighters, 1917–18; Junkers Ju 52, 1932; Fieseler Storch, 1939; Messerschmidt Me 109, 1939; Messerschmidt Me 262, the first mass-produced jet fighter, 1944; Me 163 rocket craft, 1940.
Chemistry: 16th, 17th and 18th c. laboratories (including those of Lavoisier and Liebig); matter, the atom, the molecule, chemical reactions, chemical analysis; chemical synthesis, biochemistry; 100 demonstrations of experiments; chemical apparatus (originals).
Chemical engineering: development of the chemical industry; production and processing of synthetic materials.
Music: collection of musical instruments (wind, string and plucked string instruments, musical-boxes).
Geodesy: surveying instruments and methods used in map-making and determining the size and shape of the earth.
Communications technology: development of the telegraph and telephone, radio, data processing.

Second floor

Early crafts: Ice Age painting (copy of painting in Altamira cave), ceramics, sacred art, jewellery.
Glass technology: production and processing of glass, illustrating its historical development.
Writing and printing: development of writing; writing implements and machines; relief printing, gravure printing, offset printing, silk-screen printing; reproduction camera; book-binding; paper-making.
Photography and cinematography: cameras (still and ciné), projectors.
Textile technology: development from craft to industrial production; the spindle, the loom, the spinning-wheel spinning and weaving machines.

Third floor

Space travel: rockets, satellites, ground installations.
Agricultural technology: development of agricultural implements and machinery. Indoor operations: hand-driven machinery, milking machines. Outdoor operations: machines for working the land, sowing and harvesting (first motor plough, 1907; first Bulldog tractor, 1921). Dairying, milling, distilling, brewing, sugar production.
Measurement of time: development of clocks and watches from the water-clock and the sundial to the quartz-actuated watch.
Weights and measures: development of measures and measuring apparatus for length, volume and mass.

Sixth floor

Planetarium

HF 31
HF 31

The Glypothek, a masterpiece of classical proportion

**Glyptothek (Sculpture Gallery) N17

Location
Königsplatz 3

U-Bahn
Königsplatz

Opening times
Tue., Wed., Fri.–Sun.
10 a.m.–4.30 p.m., Thu.
midday–8.30 p.m.

Conducted tours
Thu. 7 p.m.

The Glyptothek has one of the finest collections of sculpture in Europe, largely assembled in the early 19th c. by King Ludwig I, a great lover of ancient art, whose agents brought back from Egypt, Greece and Italy numerous works of Greek and Roman sculpture, including the fine figures from the pediment of the Temple of Aphaia on the island of Aegina. Since there was no suitable place to house these treasures, Leo von Klenze was commissioned to build a new gallery for them; and, using plans prepared by Karl von Fischer, he erected one of the finest and most celebrated neo-classical buildings in Germany, the Glyptothek. Laid out round a central courtyard, it is fronted by an Ionic portico. The rooms are lit from the courtyard; the exterior walls are windowless, their bareness relieved by 18 statues in niches. The Glyptothek was destroyed by bombing in 1943–44, but its valuable contents had been removed to places of safety and survived the war undamaged.
Some notable items: Apollo of Tenea, from a tomb (*c.* 560–550 B.C.); figure of a youth from Aegina, 540–530 B.C. (Room I); sleeping satyr, 2nd c. B.C. (Room II); bronze head of a victorious athlete, *c.* 420 B.C. (Room III); Tomb of Mesarete, *c.* 380 B.C. (Room IV); Aeginetan heroes fighting the Trojans, *c.* 510–480 B.C., in mature Archaic style (Rooms VII and IX); figure of Augustus, collection of Roman portrait busts (Room XI).

◀ *Shipping Hall in the German Museum*

Graphic Collection (Graphische Sammlung) N17

Location
Meiserstrasse 10

U-Bahn
Königsplatz

Opening times
Mon.–Fri. 9 a.m.–1 p.m. and 2–4.30 p.m.

The State Graphic Collection comprises 300,000 sheets of drawings and graphics, ranging in date from the 15th c. to the present day. Among the German artists represented are Altdorfer, Dürer and Elsheimer, of the Italians Fra Bartolomeo and Rembrandt among the Dutch and Flemish. The collection is particularly rich in material of the Baroque period in southern Germany (the Asam brothers, Ignaz Günther) and in 19th c. work (Klenze, Kobell, Schwind, Marées, Wilhelm Busch).

Grünwald V16

S-Bahn
Höllriegelskreuth

Tram
25

Distance
13 km (8 miles) S

The little town of Grünwald, on the right bank of the Isar a few kilometres south of Munich, is first recorded in 1291. It has the only medieval castle in the neighbourhood of Munich. Built in 1293, the castle was later used as a hunting-lodge; it now houses a local museum (Heimatmuseum; open Wed.–Sun.).
From Grünwald there are pleasant walks either up the Isar Valley to Schäftlarn (see entry) or downstream to Hellabrunn Zoo (see entry).

Hauptpost

See Head Post Office

Haus der Kunst

See State Gallery of Modern Art

Haus zur Hundskugel

See Hundskugel House

Head Post Office (Hauptpost; formerly Palais Törring-Jettenbach) O18

Location
Residenzstrasse 2

U-Bahn
Marienplatz

S-Bahn
Marienplatz

The Palais Törring-Jettenbach, now occupied by the Head Post Office, was built in 1747–54 by Ignaz Anton Gunetzrhainer. The decoration of the interior was the work of his brother Johann Baptist; the stucco-work was by Johann Baptist Zimmermann. Nine figures in the staircase hall (now in the Bavarian National Museum (see entry)) were carved by Johann Baptist Straub (1744).
In 1834 the palace was acquired by the Post Office for 180,000 florins. King Ludwig I had pressed strongly for the purchase, since, in accordance with the plans of his architect Leo von Klenze, he wanted to have a suitably imposing building with a proper colonnaded front in Max-Joseph-Platz opposite the Königsbau wing of the Residence. Between 1836 and 1839

Klenze modified the palace by adding two additional windows at each end and an open portico in front. The cost of the project was the cause of considerable outcry. Klenze had estimated the cost of the alterations at 85,000 florins, and Ludwig had repeatedly stressed that this was to be the absolute maximum; however, as a result of changes regarded as "highly necessary and advantageous", the final total cost turned out to be more than twice the estimated sum.

*Heiliggeistkirche

See Holy Ghost, Church of the

Heiligkreuzkirche

See Holy Cross Church

**Hellabrunn Zoo (Tierpark Hellabrunn) S/T16/17

Munich's Zoo at Hellabrunn is one of the most popular attractions in Bavaria. With more than 4800 animals from all parts of the world, it is the world's first geographically organised zoo (laid out in 1928). The animals, grouped according to the different parts of the world from which they come, live in open enclosures reproducing as far as possible their natural habitat. Among the Zoo's most popular features are the section devoted to the anthropoid apes (orang-utan twins), Tiger Valley, the Wolves' Wood, the Polarium, the Brown Bears' Enclosure, the Elk Bog and the houses for Asian beasts of prey (tigers, leopards, panthers). Near the principal restaurant is the Children's Zoo, with ponies and miniature donkeys.

Among the animals bred at Hellabrunn are many of the larger mammals, including the very popular anthropoid apes (gorillas, chimpanzees, orang-utans), together with giraffes, bison, hippopotamuses, antelopes, lions, panthers and jaguars. The Zoo has gained an international reputation for its success in breeding rare species threatened with extinction, including primitive wild horses, bison, white-tailed gnus, wild bantengs, Père David deer and Siberian tigers.

Great interest has also been aroused by the attempts made at Hellabrunn to breed back from primitive breeds of domestic horse to the extinct aurochs.

Location
Siebenbrunner Strasse 6

Buses
31, 52, 57

Distance
6 km (4 miles) S

Opening times
Daily 8 a.m.–6 p.m., winter 9 a.m.–5 p.m.

Conducted tours
Wed. 2 p.m.

*Hofbräuhaus O18

This world-famed beer-hall in the older part of Munich, one of the city's major tourist attractions, was established by Duke William V as long ago as 1589 in order to provide for the needs of his Court and domestic staff (Hofbräuhaus means Court Brew-House); but it was not until 1830, when the citizens of Munich were allowed for the first time to drink the excellent

Location
Platzl 9

U-Bahn
Marienplatz

The Hofbräuhaus, a world-famed centre of Bavarian conviviality

S-Bahn
Marienplatz

beer brewed for the Court, that the brewery began to operate as a beer-house. Its fame as a place of conviviality soon spread far beyond the bounds of the city, a fame enhanced by a popular song, "In München steht ein Hofbräuhaus". In 1890 the brewery was moved out to Haidhausen, and the Hofbräuhaus, rebuilt in neo-Renaissance style, became a large and busy beer-hall.
On the ground floor is the Schwemme (literally "watering-place": the equivalent, perhaps, of the public bar in an English pub), where the customers drink their beer at wooden tables scrubbed till they shine, to the accompaniment of a Bavarian brass band. On the upper floor are a number of rooms for more select company and a banner-decorated banqueting hall.
In summer beer is also served in the arcaded courtyard.

*Hofgarten (Court Garden) N18

U-Bahn
Odeonsplatz

S-Bahn
Marienplatz

The Hofgarten, a garden in the Italian style, lies on the north side of the Residence (see entry), enclosed on two sides by arcades 583 m (638 yd) long. It was laid out in its present form in 1613–17, in the time of Duke Maximilian I, and has undergone no significant alteration since then.
In the centre of the gardens stands the Hofgarten temple, a twelve-sided pavilion with a low domed roof (1615; attributed to Heinrich Schön the Elder). The graceful bronze figure on the roof (by Hubert Gerhard, 1594) was given new attributes to make it a symbol of Bavaria by Hans Krumper. On the east side of the Hofgarten is the ruin of the Army Museum (see entry).

Fountain in the Hofgarten; to rear the Theatinerkirche

Holy Cross Church (Heiligkreuzkirche)

This Late Gothic parish and pilgrimage church, built in the 15th c., was remodelled in Baroque style in the 17th and 18th c. (stucco-work of 1626 in nave, of 1749 in choir). The tower was given an octagonal superstructure in 1626, a new onion dome in 1749. The church contains a valuable carved Crucifix (Romanesque, *c.* 1180) from Seeon Monastery in the Chiemgau. The statues of Christ and the Mater Dolorosa on the pilasters along the wall were the work of A. Fassbinder (1708). Tabernacle of 1700.

Location
Forstenrieder Allee 180A, Forstenried

Buses
35, 65, 66

Tram
16

*Holy Ghost, Church of the (Heiliggeistkirche) O18

This Gothic hall-church, originally belonging to the Hospice of the Holy Ghost (14th c.), was remodelled in 1724–30 by Johann Georg Ettenhofer (vaulting, refacing of pillars); in the interior can be seen fine Rococo frescoes and stucco ornament by the Asam brothers. After the demolition of the hospice buildings, in 1885, Franz Löwel added three bays at the west end of the church and gave it an imposing neo-Baroque façade. The church suffered severe damage during the Second World War and its interior furnishings were largely destroyed; extensive rebuilding and restoration was carried out after the war.

Of the original Gothic church there remain only the choir buttresses and the north wall of the nave. The tower (1729–30)

Location
Tal 77

U-Bahn
Marienplatz

S-Bhan
Marienplatz

has a lantern dome of characteristic Munich type. The neo-Baroque façade shows a skilful use of elements borrowed from Viscardi's Trinity Church (see entry).
The interior is aisled, with an ambulatory round the choir. The nave is barrel-vaulted, with small vaults over the windows. The aisles have groined vaulting.
Notable features of the interior:
In the porch (to left and right of main entrance), parts of the bronze Tomb of Duke Ferdinand of Bavaria (by Hans Krumper, 1608).
The High Altar (by Nikolaus Stuber, 1730), with an altar-piece by Ulrich Loth, "Descent of the Holy Ghost" (1661), and two flanking figures of angels by Johann Georg Greiff (1729–30).
A series of wall-paintings by Peter Horemans of the Seven Gifts of the Holy Spirit (1725), in the south aisle.
A Late Gothic Crucifix (1510) in the Chapel of the Cross (Kreuzkapelle).
Altar of Our Lady, with the Hammerthal Madonna (15th c.), half-way along the north aisle.

Hundskugel House (Haus zur Hundskugel) O18

Location
Hackenstrasse 10

S-Bahn and U-Bahn
Marienplatz

This 18th c. burgher's house was created in 1741 by the conversion of an older barn. From 1741 to 1777 it was occupied by the sculptor Johann Baptist Straub, and later by his son-in-law Roman Boos.
Over the left-hand entrance door is a relief by Boos (six dogs playing with a sphere) illustrating the name of the house ("At the Sign of the Dogs' Sphere").

Hundskugel Inn (Gaststätte zur Hundskugel) O18

Location
Hotterstrasse 18

U-Bahn and S-Bahn
Marienplatz

This unpretentious corner house contains Munich's oldest inn (first mentioned 1440). Over the door is a shallow oriel; in the gable, above a beam for a hoist, are small round-headed windows.

Hunting Museum (Jagdmuseum) O18

Location
Neuhauser Strasse 53

U-Bahn
Marienplatz

S-Bahn
Marienplatz

Opening times
Daily 9.30 a.m.–5 p.m.; also Mon. 7–10 p.m.

The German Hunting and Fishing Museum is housed in the Augustinian Church of St John the Evangelist and St John the Baptist, which was built in the late 13th c., enlarged at the beginning of the 14th c., remodelled in Baroque style (vaulting, stucco-work) in 1618–21 (the first Munich church to be so treated) and secularised in 1802.
The museum (founded in 1934) illustrates the history of hunting in a variety of exhibits and displays, including preserved specimens of game animals, stabbing and cutting weapons and firearms of three centuries, hunting equipment, hunting pictures, graphic art (drawings by Ridinger), printed matter and sumptuous hunting sleighs of the Baroque, Rococo and Empire periods.
A series of 44 dioramas (by E. Oberle) show groups of animals in their natural environment.

The Isartor

In the fishing section are specimens of all freshwater fishes, fossils of primitive fishes, illustrations of various species of fish and fishing equipment from the Stone Age to modern times.

Ignaz Günther's House (Ignaz-Günther-Haus) O18

This house, the dwelling and studio of the sculptor Ignaz Günther (1725–75), was opened in 1977, after extensive restoration, as a memorial to the great 18th c. artist.
On the Oberanger frontage note the gable, of characteristic Munich type. The interior preserves an old barrel-vaulted timber roof and a Jacob's ladder leading up through two floors.
The rooms now house an exhibition illustrating Günther's work.
The upper floor is occupied by offices of the Municipal Museum (see entry).

Location
Unterer Anger 30,
Oberanger 11

U-Bahn
Sendlinger-Tor-Platz

S-Bahn
Marienplatz

*Isartor (Isar Gate) O18

The Isartor, the only one of Munich's town gates that has preserved its gate-tower, formed part of the fortifications erected by Ludwig the Bavarian in the first half of the 14th c.
The mural depicting Ludwig's victorious entry after the Battle of Ampfingen in 1322 was the work of Caspar Neher (1835).
The Isartor now houses the Valentin Museum (see entry), a bar and a museum of folk-singing.

Location
Tal, Isartorplatz

S-Bahn
Isartor

*Kammerspiele (Theatre) O18

Location
Maximilianstrasse 26–28

Trams
14, 19

This is the only Art Nouveau theatre in Germany. The oval auditorium (seating 727), with stalls, balcony and proscenium boxes, is decorated in a festive combination of red, green and gold. Every detail in decoration and furnishings is Art Nouveau (in Germany known as Jugendstil).
The curtain is a reconstruction of the original, which was designed by Richard Riemerschmid.
The foyers and entrance lobby are equally consistent in style. The original colouring has been restored – brown and red in the lobby, blue and green in the ground-floor foyer, light grey, yellow and white in the upper foyer.
Built and decorated in 1900–01 by Max Littmann and Richard Riemerschmid, the theatre was renovated in 1937 and again in 1950, in a fashion that destroyed its uniformity of style and decoration; in 1970–71, however, it was restored to its original form.
The repertoire of the theatre and its associated Theatre Workshop (Werkraumtheater) ranges from classical drama by way of classic modern plays to experimental contemporary works.

Karlsplatz

See Stachus

Karolinenplatz N17

U-Bahn
Odeonsplatz, Königsplatz

The Karolinensplatz, Munich's first star-shaped open space, was laid out in 1809–12 to the plans of Karl von Fischer, who took as his model the Place de l'Etoile in Paris. The obelisk (by Leo von Klenze) in the middle of the square commemorates the 30,000 Bavarian soldiers who fell in the Russian campaign of 1812.
The uniform neo-classical character of the square has unfortunately been damaged by later building.

*Königsplatz N17

U-Bahn
Königsplatz

This monumental neo-classical square – Munich's forum of the arts, the counterpart of its forum of the sciences in Ludwigstrasse – was designed in 1811 by Karl von Fischer and surrounded by Leo von Klenze's Glyptothek (see entry) and Propylaea (see entry) and the building by Georg Friedrich Ziebland opposite the Glyptothek which now houses the National Collection in Antiquities (see entry).
Originally laid out in grass, the square was given its present stone paving during the Nazi period. There has been much controversy among experts over the appropriateness of this: to some it is objectionable as a former Nazi parade-ground, while others applaud it as giving the Königsplatz the atmosphere of a piazza.

Künstlerhaus (Artists' House) O17

The Künstlerhaus was built by Gabriel von Seidl in 1892–1900 as a meeting-place for the leading Munich artists of the day. It is a tall square building with curving gables, with two lower wings enclosing a courtyard in front of it. The lavish interior decoration, only part of which has survived in its original state, was mainly designed by Lenbach.
The Künstlerhaus is now occupied by the Mövenpick restaurant and a small theatre.

Location
Lenbachplatz 8

S-Bahn
Karlsplatz

Lenbachplatz N/O17

The Lenbachplatz is a typical example of turn-of-the-century urban design. The buildings are grouped with a view to picturesque effect, without any precise plan or close relationship to one another. To the south the square opens into the Karlsplatz (Stachus (see entry)); on its west side are the massive Old Law Courts (see entry) and the entrance to the Old Botanic Gardens (see entry), with Herigoyen's neo-classical gate; and on the north is the palatial building occupied by the Bavarian Stock Exchange (Visitors' Gallery open Mon.–Fri. 11.30 a.m.–1.30 p.m.). At the north-east corner of the square is the Wittelsbach Fountain (see entry).

U-Bahn
Hauptbahnhof

S-Bahn
Karlsplatz

*Lenbach Villa and Municipal (Städtische Galerie) N17

The villa once occupied by the celebrated 19th c. painter Franz von Lenbach (see Notable Personalities) has since 1929 housed Munich's Municipal Gallery.
The house was built for Lenbach and, with his collaboration, by Gabriel von Seidl in 1887–91, in a style modelled on an Italian country villa of the Renaissance period. The artist's studios were in the south wing, built in 1891 and linked with the main building in 1912. An annex was added on the south side in 1972.
The extensive collections of the Municipal Gallery embrace the history of art in Munich from the Gothic period to the present day. They are particularly rich in works of the 19th c. (Lenbach, Corinth, Slevogt) and 20th c. (Marc, Macke, Kandinsky, Klee).
Ground floor: works from about 1920 to the present day (Klee, Schrimpf, Caspar-Filser, Zimmermann, etc.); Munich painting of the Gothic and Baroque periods (including a famous portrait of Countess Holnstein by Desmarées).
Upper floor: Munich painters of the Romantic school and landscapists of the first half of the 19th c. (Spitzweg, Lenbach, Defregger, Corinth, Slevogt, etc.); the famous Kladinsky Collection (Gabriele Münter Donation), with some 500 paintings, drawings, water-colours and prints; works of the Blauer Reiter school (Marc, Macke, Münter, Jawlensky, etc.).

Location
Luisenstrasse 33 and 35

U-Bahn
Königsplatz

Opening times
Tue.–Sun. 10 a.m.–6 p.m.

The Künstlerhaus in Lenbachplatz

The Lenbach Villa, home of the celebrated 19th c. painter Franz von Lenbach

Leopoldstrasse

J19–M18/19

The Leopoldstrasse continues the line of the Ludwigstrasse (see entry) northward from the Siegestor (see entry) to the square known as the Münchener Freiheit and beyond. It is both a major traffic artery and a favourite promenade for the inhabitants of Schwabing (see entry). Numerous cafés tempt the passer-by to linger; and on summer evenings, by the light of candles and oil-lamps, artists, students and miscellaneous hawkers offer for sale a wide variety of arts and crafts, trinkets and trash: water-colours and oil-paintings, leather goods, articles in silver-ware, carvings and other items of varying degrees of utility.

U-Bahn
Giselastrasse,
Münchener Freiheit

Leuchtenberg-Palais (Leuchtenberg Palace)

N18

This neo-classical mansion, built by Leo von Klenze in 1816–21 on the model of the Palozzo Farnese in Rome, set the pattern for the development of the Ludwigstrasse. Count von Leuchtenberg was Napoleon's stepson Eugène de Beauharnais, for a time Viceroy of Italy, who married a daughter of King Maximillian I Joseph of Bavaria. The palace, rebuilt after suffering severe damage during the Second World War, became the headquarters of the Bavarian Ministry of Finance in 1966.

Location
Odeonsplatz 4

U-Bahn
Odeonsplatz

*Ludwigskirche

N18

The Ludwigskirche, a parish church as well as the University church, was built between 1829 and 1844, during the development of the northern section of the Ludwigstrasse. It was designed by Friedrich von Gärtner, an architect who took his inspiration from the Romantic school, at the behest of King Ludwig I.

The church suffered damage during the Second World War but was later restored.

The church's relationship to its surroundings is skilfully contrived. The façade with its widely spaced towers is impressive when seen at an angle from the Ludwigstrasse, and also makes an effective termination of Schellingstrasse. Gärtner also established a relationship between his church and the Baroque Theatinerkirche at the south end of the Ludwigstrasse and on the opposite side, taking over from that church its cruciform plan (with small transepts) and the pattern of the façade with its twin towers.

On the façade, in circular niches above the porch, are figures (by Ludwig Schwanthaler, 1832–35) of Christ and the Four Evangelists. The round-headed arches of the porch are continued in the arcading on either side which links the church with two plain square houses, the presbytery on the south side and a house on the north side once occupied by Ludwig von Gärtner and now the offices of the University architect's department.

The interior of the church is dominated by a large fresco of the

Location
Ludwistrasse 20

U-Bahn
Universität

Last Judgment on the chancel wall, a work by the Romantic painter Peter Cornelius which gave a fresh impulse to 19th c. monumental painting. It is the world's largest mural painting after Michelangelo's "Last Judgment" in the Sistine Chapel. The frescoes in the transepts and crossing were also Cornelius's work.

*Ludwigstrasse M/N18

U-Bahn
Odeonsplatz, Universität

The Ludwigstrasse is one of Munich's two great monumental avenues (the other being the Brienner Strasse (see entry), extending for some three-quarters of a mile from the Odeonsplatz in the direction of Schwabing (see entry). It was laid out at the behest of King Ludwig I as a prestige street worthy of his kingdom. The general plan of the Ludwigstrasse was prepared by Leo von Klenze, who also designed the buildings in the southern part of the street in a rigorously neo-classical style modelled on Early Renaissance architecture in Italy. The northern section was built by Klenze's successor as Court Architect, Friedrich von Gärtner, an adherent of the Romantic Christian school of architecture who preferred neo-Romanesque.

This change in architectural style, however, did not detract from the overall impression of uniformity, for Gärtner held firmly to Klenze's basic conception of broad-fronted buildings, depending for effect on their façades, and narrow streets coming in on the sides. "Europe's most monumental street" (Wölfflin) has thus been able to preserve its unity, with only a few façades altered from the original plan.

The terminal point of the street at the south end is the Feldherrnhalle (see entry), at the north end the Siegestor (see entry). The architectural pattern was set by the Leuchtenberg-Palais (1816-21; see entry). The last building erected in the Ludwigstrasse by Klenze was the old Ministry of War, now occupied by the Bavarian State Archives. Friedrich von Gärtner designed the State Library (No. 16; see entry), the Ludwigskirche (No. 20; see entry) and the University (photograph, p. 65).

Luitpoldpark K17/18

Location
Karl-Theodor-Strasse

U-Bahn
Scheidplatz

The Luitpoldpark was established in 1911 by citizens of Munich, who presented Prince Luitpold, the popular Prince Regent, with 90 lime trees on his 90th birthday and planted them in rows on the western borders of Schwabing (see entry). Later a wide range of recreational facilities for sports and recreation were provided in this area. After the Second World War the Schwabinger Schuttberg, a huge and unsightly mound of rubble from buildings destroyed by bombing, was landscaped and planted to make it a pleasant hill and viewpoint.

On the west side of the park is the Bamberger Haus (1913), in which the architect incorporated part of the Baroque façade of the Böttingerhaus, an old Bamberg mansion which had been demolished. It is to be brought back into use as a garden café – a project which will please many Munich people.

The Ludwigstrasse, with the Ludwigskirche (right) and the Theatinerkirche (left) ▶

Lustheim Palace (Schloss Lustheim)

See Schleissheim

*Marienplatz O18

U-Bahn
Marienplatz

S-Bahn
Marienplatz

The Marienplatz has been Munich's central square since the foundation of the town. For many centuries, until 1807, it was the market square, and during the Middle Ages it was frequently the venue of knightly tournaments. The present buildings date mainly from the 19th and 20th c.

The dominant feature of the square is the New Town Hall (see entry), a building of overpowering proportions which occupies the whole of its north side. At the east end of the square stands the Old Town Hall (see entry), with its reconstructed tower. The massive modern department store at the south-west corner is one of the most controversial of the new buildings in Munich's old town.

In the centre of the square rises the Mariensäule (Virgin's Column), erected in 1638 in thanksgiving for the preservation of Munich and Landshut during the Swedish occupation (1632). The red marble column bears a gilded figure of the Virgin as Patroness of Bavaria with the Infant Jesus and a crescent moon, originally carved by Hubert Gerhard for the High Altar of the Frauenkirche. The four winged figures of children (probably by Georg Petel) on the base are respectively combating plague, war, famine and heresy.

At the north-east corner of the square is the Fischbrunnen (Fish Fountain), recently erected here, with bronze figures from an earlier fountain of 1865. Until 1901 this was the scene, each year on Shrove Tuesday, of a light-hearted event known as the Metzgersprung (Butchers' Leap). Apprentice butchers were ceremonially released from their indentures, and were then required, wearing sheepskins, to jump into the fountain basin. They then threw nuts into the crowd, and splashed the small boys who ran up to get them.

Marstallmuseum

See Nymphenburg

Matthäuskirche

See St Matthew's Church

Maxburg N/O17/18

Location
Pacellistrasse, Lenbachplatz

Towards the end of the 16th c. Heinrich Schön the Elder built a stronghold for Duke William V, the Wilhelminische Veste, on a site previously occupied by 54 burghers' houses. His successor Duke (later Elector) Maximilian I made this his

The Marienplatz, with the New Town Hall (to rear, the towers of the Frauenkirche) ▶

S-Bahn
Karlsplatz

residence, and it became known as the Maxburg (Max's Castle). Of the original structure only the tower on the north front survives. The replacement erected in the 1950s, following the general plan of the Maxburg but preserving nothing of the spirit of the original, is occupied by the police and criminal authorities. In the courtyard is the Moses Fountain (by Joseph Henselmann, 1955), which depicts the Prophet standing on a tall crag and striking water out of the rock.

* Maximilianeum — O19

Location
Max-Planck-Strasse 1

Trams
14, 19

Bus
53

The Maximilianeum, seat of the Bavarian Landtag and Senate, closes the vista at the east end of the Maximilianstrasse. This conspicuous Munich landmark (floodlit at night) on the east bank of the Isar was built by Friedrich Bürklein between 1857 and 1874. The long main front was originally designed in Gothic style with pointed arches, but at the request of Maximilian II the architect substituted round-headed arches in Renaissance style, since Gothic arches were felt to be unsuitable for a long series of windows. The broad central block, decorated with semicircular mosaics on a gold ground and topped by a figure of an angel, is flanked on both sides by open arcades.
The Maximilianeum was originally conceived as a picture gallery and a training institution for civil servants; and the Maximilianeum Foundation (Stiftung Maximilianeum) still awards scholarships providing free board and lodging for gifted students – including, only in recent years, female students.

* Maximilianstrasse — O18/19

U-Bahn
Odeonsplatz

The Maximilianstrasse, the third of Munich's 19th c. prestige streets, starts from the Max-Joseph-Platz and runs east through the Lehel and Haidhausen districts, linking them with the old town. It was designed by Friedrich Bürklein.
In contrast to the rigorously controlled architecture of his father's Ludwigstrasse (see entry), Maximilian II wanted his show street to have a looser structure: public buildings, shops, hotels, restaurants and gardens were to alternate with one another. This concept, however, was realised only in the western part of the street; the eastern section, like the Ludwigstrasse, consisted predominantly of buildings of imposing monumentality.
For the Maximilianstrasse, at Maximilian's behest, a new "uniform architectural style appropriate to the circumstances of our time" was devised – the Maximilianic style, a synthesis of various styles of the past with a predominance of Gothic elements.
Half-way along its course the unity of the Maximilianstrasse is destroyed by its intersection with the Altstadtring, the ring of wide boulevards round the old town. In the western half are the Kammerspiele (see entry (Theatre)) and the world-famous Vier Jahreszeiten (Four Seasons) Hotel (1856–58). Between the intersection with the Altstadtring and the Isar, in the eastern

The Maximilianeum, seat of the Bavarian Landtag, seen from the Isar

The Maximilianstrasse, a 19th c. prestige street.

half of the Maximilianstrasse, are the offices of the regional administration of Upper Bavaria (Regierung von Oberbayern), the Museum of Ethnology (see entry) and the Maxmonument (see entry).
A prominent landmark at the eastern end of the Maximilianstrasse is the Maximilianeum (see entry).

Maxmonument (Monument to King Maximilian II) O19

Location
Maximilianstrasse

Trams
14, 19, 20

This monument commemorates Maximilian II (1848–64), who built the Maximilianstrasse. The bronze figure of the King stands on a high base of red marble, on which are bronze figures symbolising the virtues of Statecraft and four children bearing the coats of arms of the four Bavarian peoples (Bavaria, Swabia, Franconia and Rhineland-Palatinate).

**Michaelskirche

See St Michael's Church

Mint (Münze) O18

Location
Hofgraben 4

U-Bahn
Marienplatz

S-Bahn
Marienplatz

The building which has housed the Bavarian Mint since 1809 was originally erected by the Court Architect, Wilhelm Egkl, in 1563–67 to accommodate Duke Albert V's art collection and library and the Court stables. Consisting of four wings enclosing an inner courtyard, it was linked by arcades with the Alter Hof (see entry (Old Court)) and the Neuveste (New Castle: see Residence). In the 19th c. it was given a neo-classical west front and a neo-Gothic north front (by the addition of arcades of pointed arches).
The courtyard, measuring 32 m (105 ft) by 12 m (40 ft), has been preserved in its original form, with arcaded galleries on all four sides on each floor level. It is of importance as the first introduction into Munich of the Court architecture of the Italian Renaissance, but it is no mere copy. The architect was not concerned to achieve a strictly schematic arrangement of the columns and arcades, but the building he produced is an informal but, nevertheless, finely proportioned masterpiece.
It is planned to open the courtyard to the public, but there is no admission to the interior of the building.

Modern Art, State Gallery of

See State Gallery of Modern Art

Montgelas-Palais O18

Location
Promenadeplatz 2

This palace in mature neo-classical style was built by Herigoyen for Count Maximilian Joseph von Montgelas, who is regarded as the creator of modern Bavaria (having preserved the independence of Bavaria between the two great powers, Austria and France, and established a central administration). In 1971–72 the palace was almost completely rebuilt and taken over by the Bayrischer Hof Hotel. Some rooms have survived in their original form.

U-Bahn
Marienplatz, Odeonsplatz

S-Bahn
Karlsplatz, Marienplatz

*Municipal Museum (Stadtmuseum) O18

The Municipal Museum is housed in the old municipal Arsenal (a gabled building of the 15th c. with corner turrets which has preserved its vaulted Gothic hall), the adjoining Marstallgebäude (Court Stables; 15th c., reconstructed in 1977–78) and a 20th c. extension. The Museum, opened in 1888, gives a comprehensive view of the municipal and cultural history of Munich. The collections on permanent display are supplemented by periodic special exhibitions.

Location
Sankt-Jakobs-Platz 1

U-Bahn
Marienplatz

S-Bahn
Marienplatz

Opening times
Tue.–Sat. 9 a.m.–4.30 p.m., Sun. and pub. hol. 10 a.m.–6 p.m.

The ground floor is devoted to medieval Munich. In the Maruska Room are the figures of Morisco dancers carved by Erasmus, Grasser about 1480 for the ballroom of the Old Town Hall (see entry). Dainty, earthy and grotesque, they are notable examples of middle-class art of the Gothic period.
The Morisco (morris) dance, imported from Moorish Spain and spread throughout Europe by itinerant singers and musicians, depicted the competition by costumed dancers for the favour of a fair lady.
In the same room are coats of arms (also by Grasser) carved for the barrel-vaulted roof of the municipal Council Chamber, including one with the "Münchner Kindl" (the figure of a child which is Munich's emblem), and a representation of the crescent moon with the sun in the likeness of an old woman's head.
In the well-preserved Gothic vaulted hall of the Arsenal are weapons borne by the old Municipal Guard (Stadtwehr; 15th–16th c.).
German Brewing Museum: historical development of brewing; bottles, tankards, glasses, paintings and drawings.
Photographic and Film Museum (first floor): material illustrating the development of photographic and film techniques; exhibitions of photographs; film shows (daily at 6.30 p.m.); the laboratory of the physicist and astronomer Joseph Fraunhofer, with his optical apparatus.
On the second floor are 20 rooms from Munich houses, with period furnishings, ranging from Baroque to Art Nouveau.
Puppet Theatre Collection (third floor): one of the largest collections of its kind, with some 40,000 puppets and shadow-play figures, mainly from European countries.
On the fourth floor is Germany's largest collection of musical instruments, with primitive, exotic, ancient, medieval and modern percussion, string, plucked string and wind instruments from all over the world and a recorded archive of folk-music from non-European countries.

Münze

See Mint

Auditorium of the National Theatre

* National Theatre (Nationaltheater) O18

Location
Max-Joseph-Platz 2

U-Bahn
Marienplatz

S-Bahn
Marienplatz

The National Theatre, Munich's world-famous opera house, originally known as the Royal Court and National Theatre, was built by Karl von Fischer in neo-classical style in 1811–18; burned down in 1823, it was reopened in 1825. It was destroyed again during the Second World War (when the Opera moved to the Prinzregententheater) but was rebuilt in its original form and reopened in 1963. It is also known as the New Residence Theatre.
The portico with its Corinthian columns and the two triangular pediments are reminiscent of a Greek temple. In the pediment of the portico are Apollo and the Muses (by Bręnninger, 1972), in that of the tall main structure a coloured glass mosaic on a gold ground depicting Pegasus with the Horae (by Ludwig Schwanthaler). The interior is also predominantly Greek in style – the entrance lobby Doric, the staircase Ionic, the Royal Foyer Corinthian. The auditorium with its five tiers of seating is decorated in red, ivory, dove-blue and gold.
During the reign of Ludwig II, a fervent admirer of Wagner, the first performances of "Tristan and Isolde" (1865), the "Mastersingers" (1868), "Rhine Gold" (1869) and the "Valkyrie" (1870) were given in the National Theatre. Among the conductors who have directed operas here have been Hans von Bülow, Bruno Walter, Clemens Krauss, Hans Knappertsbusch and Joseph Keilberth.
The National Theatre now ranks among the world's leading opera houses. The most brilliant event in the theatrical season is the Munich Opera Festival, held annually in summer.

** Neue Pinakothek (New Picture Gallery) M18

Location
Barer Strasse 29
(entrance in Theresienstrasse)

U-Bahn
Theresienstrasse

Tram
18

Bus
53

Opening times
Wed.–Sun. 9 a.m.–4.30 p.m.,
Tue. 9 a.m.–4.30 p.m. and 7–9 p.m.

Closed
Mon.

The original Neue Pinakothek, built between 1846 and 1853, suffered heavy damage during the Second World War and had to be pulled down. Thereafter for many years the gallery's collection of late 18th c. and 19th c. work was housed in the Haus der Kunst. The new gallery, standing opposite the Alte Pinakothek and contrasting with it, was designed by Alexander von Branca and built in 1975–80. It is 160 m (525 ft) long by 100 m (330 ft) deep, and is the largest museum built in Germany since the last War.

In spite of its great size the building does not have a ponderous effect. Its bulk is relieved by the rows of narrow round-headed windows, the high glass wall of the entrance hall on its south side (in which the round-arched motif is continued), the pent-roof windows, set back above one another, and the angled end walls and staircases with copper roofs. Branca's use of traditional architectural elements like round-headed arches, normally taboo in modern architecture, reflected his desire to get away from what he called the pure schematism of the modern style.

The building consists of two ranges of rooms: the gallery range, with 22 rooms and 11 cabinets, contains the collections of the

Neue Pinakothek

KR Karl Rottmann

A, B Special exhibition, graphic art

R restaurant and café (in basement)

1, 2 Art about 1800
3 Early Romantic period
4 Court art under Ludwig I
5 German neo-classicists in Rome
6 Georg Schäfer Collection
7 Nazarenes
8, 9 Biedermeier
10, 11 Late Romantic period and Realism
12 Kaulbach's sketches for frescoes on the original building
13 Historical and genre painting about 1870
14 Painting of the Gründerzeit (early 1870s)
15 Hans von Marées
16 Anselm Feuerbach, Arnold Böcklin, Hans Thoma
17 Leibl and his group
18 French Impressionists
19 Cézanne, Gauguin, Van Gogh
20 Social Realism of the 1880s and 1890s
21 German Impressionists
21a The Secession
22 Symbolism and Art Nouveau

Neue Pinakothek, while the western part houses the offices of the Directorate of the Bavarian State Picture Collections, a library, photographic laboratories and the Doerner Institute for the Scientific Investigation and Restoration of Works of Art.
The Neue Pinakothek possesses some 550 pictures and 50 works of sculpture, ranging from Rococo to Art Nouveau. Its greatest strength lies in European painting of the 19th c.
Notable early 19th c. works:
Kobell, "Siege of Kosel" (1808), "Isar Landscape" (1819), "View of the Tegernsee" (1833); Friedrich, "Summer" (1808), "Landscape in the Riesengebirge" (*c.* 1815); Spitzweg, "The Poor Poet" (1839); Schwind, "The Visit" (1852), "Coachman Kronos" (*c.* 1854).
Important works of the later 19th c.:
Manet, "Breakfast in the Studio" (1868–69); Monet, "The Bridge at Argenteuil" (1874); Degas, "Woman ironing"; Cézanne, "Self-Portrait" (*c.* 1880); Stuck, "Sin" (1893); Klimt, "Portrait of Margarethe Stonborough-Wittgenstein".

New Collection (State Museum of Applied Art) (Neue Sammlung, Staatliches Museum für angewandte Kunst) N19

Location
Prinzregentenstrasse 3

Buses
53, 55

Tram
20

Opening times
Tue.–Sun. 10 a.m.–5 p.m.

The New Collection – officially the State Museum of Applied Art – occupies the west wing of the Bavarian National Museum (see entry). The collection was founded in 1925 as a museum of modern applied art, but now devotes itself to the collection and presentation of objects of any period which are "formative of taste and of exemplary value for well-designed product forms". The collection includes textiles, posters, ceramics, porcelain, everyday objects of all kinds, furniture, glass, lamps and metalware. Owing to shortage of space only a selection of exhibits can be shown in special exhibitions at any one time.

New Law Courts (Neuer Justizpalast) N17

Location
Prielmayerstrasse 5

This plain brick neo-Gothic building with clock-towers and stepped gables was built by Friedrich von Thiersch in 1906–08. It reflects the fashion, current at the time of its construction, for reviving Northern architectural forms, in sharp contrast to the adjoining Old Law Courts (see entry).

*New Town Hall (Neues Rathaus) O18

Location
Marienplatz 8

U-Bahn
Marienplatz

S-Bahn
Marienplatz

In the mid 19th c. the municipal council resolved to build a new Town Hall to provide much-needed additional office space. A site was cleared by the demolition of 24 older buildings, including the hall in which the Bavarian Estates had met from 1554 to 1807, and a new building was designed by Georg Hauberisser. It was erected in three stages – first the brick-built eastern part (1867–74), then the extension to the rear (1889–92) and finally the western half, in limestone, with the 85 m (280 ft) high tower, which vies with the towers of the

Mechanical figures in the Town Hall tower: above, the wedding of William V; below, the Schäfflertanz ▶

Opening times
Carillon: daily at 11 a.m., May–Oct. also at 5 p.m.
Tower: Mon.–Fri. 8 a.m.–3.45 p.m., Sat., Sun. and pub. hol. 10 a.m.–6 p.m.

Frauenkirche as Munich's best-known landmark.
The main front, looking on to the Marienplatz, is decorated with a profusion of figures and ornaments – Bavarian dukes, electors and kings, fabulous creatures, saints, Munich types and characters.
The world-famous carillon and display by mechanical figures is the fourth largest in Europe. Every day at 11 a.m. (and from May to October also at 5 p.m.) the bells play folk-tunes and the figures enact scenes from the history of Munich – the wedding of Duke William V and Renata (Renée) of Lorraine in 1568, with a jousting-match in which the Bavarian knight wins (upper figures), and the Schäfflertanz, which is danced every seven years in thanksgiving for the ending of the plague of 1515–17 (lower figures). In the evening (at nine o'clock in summer and seven in winter) there appear in the oriels on the seventh tier a night-watchman blowing his horn (left) and an angel of peace blessing the emblem of Munich, the Münchner Kindl (right). Photograph, p. 75.
From the middle gallery of the 12-storey tower there are extensive views over the city.

**Nymphenburg Palace (Schloss Nymphenburg) L/M13

Bus
41

Tram
12

Opening times
May–Sep., Tue.–Sun. 9 a.m.–12.30 p.m. and 1.30–5 p.m.; Oct.–Apr. 10 a.m.–12.30 p.m. and 1.30–4 p.m.

Nymphenburg Palace, the summer residence of the Wittelsbach Electors of Bavaria, is Germany's largest Baroque palace, with a total length of 685 m (2250 ft). Begun in 1664, it was enlarged in symmetrical fashion in later building phases. The first part to be built (by Agostino Barelli and Enrico Zuccalli, 1664–75) was the cube-shaped central block with its wide double staircase. In the second stage (1702–16, with an interruption during the War of the Spanish Succession) Antonio Viscardi added the two lateral pavilions, also cube-shaped, and linked them with the main building by open arcades. Then in 1715 Joseph Effner produced a plan for further extensions, on the basis of which the main buildings were extended in 1719–39 and the semicircular range to the east (the Schlossrondell) was built between 1728 and 1758.
The most notable features of the interior are the Stone Hall (Steinerner Saal) in the central block, the ceiling-painting by Johann Baptist and Franz Zimmermann, "Nymphs paying homage to the goddess Flora" (1756–57), a masterpiece of Bavarian Rococo, and stucco-work by Feichtmayr after sketches by Cuvilliés.

Marstallmuseum

Opening times
Tue.–Sun. 9 a.m.–midday and 1–5 p.m.; winter 10 a.m.– midday and 1–4 p.m.

The former Court Stables (Marstall) in the south wing of the palace now house the Marstallmuseum, with a collection of coaches, etc., which is rivalled only by museums in Lisbon and Vienna. The exhibits include state coaches and sleighs which belonged to Bavarian electors and kings, harness, saddles and accoutrements, pictures and drawings. Particularly notable items, sumptuously decorated, are the coronation coach (1740–41) of Elector Charles Albert (later Emperor Charles VII), richly carved, coronation coaches of 1813 and 1818 (carving by Friedrich Schwanthaler) and the wedding coach for Ludwig II's wedding, which did not take place.

Nymphenburg Porcelain Manufactory

At the north end of the Schlossrondell is the Nymphenburg Porcelain Manufactory (Porzellanmanufaktur), founded in

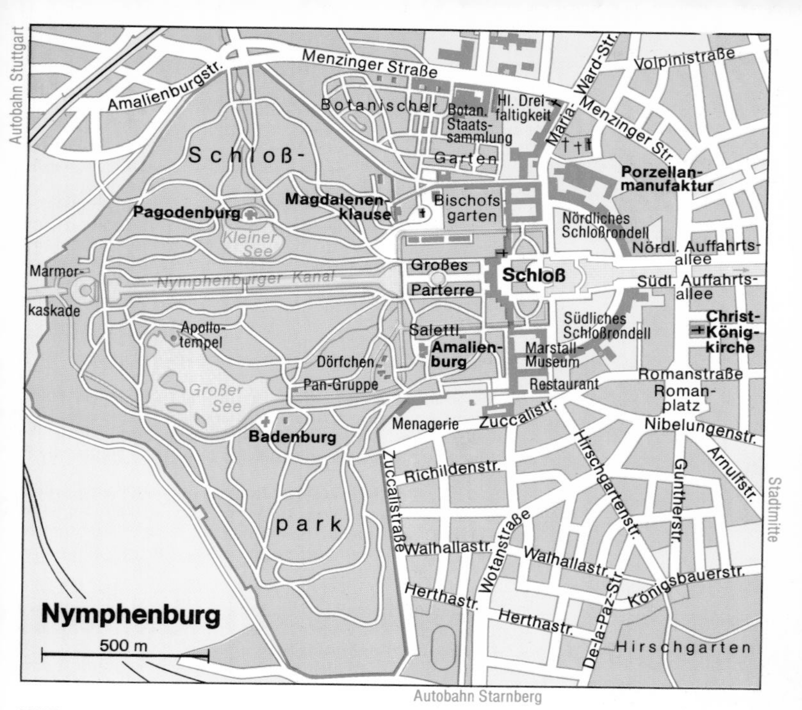

1747 and installed here in 1761. The Rococo creations of its first designer, Franz Anton Bustelli (1754–63), brought it a high reputation, which it has continued to enjoy by maintaining the old traditions.
The showrooms are open to the public.

*Nymphenburg Park — L/M 11/12

Nymphenburg Park, one of the finest landscaped gardens in Germany, was originally laid out in 1675 in Baroque style; during the 18th c. it was enlarged and redesigned in the French manner; and in the early 19th c. Ludwig von Sckell landscaped it in the English style, but left unchanged the large parterre and the canal of the Baroque layout.
On the garden side of the palace is the large Baroque parterre (Grosses Parterre), which was ornamented in 1770 with marble statues of ancient legendary figures (by Auliczek and Boos; some designed by Straub and Günther). The fountain in the centre, with a jet 10 m (33 ft) high, is still worked by a machine invented by Joseph Bader (1803–04), a remarkable technical achievement for its day; it can be seen in the Orangery on the north side of the parterre. The cascade (Marmorkaskade) at the west end of the canal was constructed by Joseph Effner and faced with marble by François Cuvilliés; the marble statues represent figures from Greek legend and mythology,

while the recumbent figures are apparenty symbols of the Danube and the Isar (by de Groff, Volpini and Boos).

Amalienburg

Opening times
May–Sep., Tue.–Sun.
9 a.m.–12.30 p.m. and 1.30–5 p.m.; Oct.–Apr., 10 a.m.–12.30 p.m. and 1.30–4 p.m.

This little single-storey hunting-lodge was built by François Cuvilliés in 1734–39 for Maria Amalia, Charles Albert's wife. During a hunt she stationed herself on the platform on the roof and shot at the game which was driven past her by beaters.
The masterly way in which architecture, decoration and furnishings are attuned to one another makes the Amalienburg Germany's finest example of a mini-palace of the Rococo period. The interior decoration was the work of Johann Baptist Zimmermann (stucco-work), Joachim Dietrich (carving) and Dutch craftsmen.
Unique in design and colouring is the circular Hall of Mirrors (Spiegelsaal), decorated with hunting symbols in silver on a blue ground. In the Rest Room (Ruhezimmer), which is decorated in silver and yellow, are portraits of Charles Ablert and his wife in riding costume (by Georges Desmarées). The Hunting Room (Jagdzimmer), also in silver and yellow, has hunting pictures by G. Horemans and pictures of animals by F. Hamilton.
Also worth seeing are the Dogs' Room (Hundekammer), which is decorated with paintings on hunting themes and contains gun-presses with beds for hunting-dogs, and the Kitchen (Küche), which is entirely faced with blue and white and coloured Dutch tiles.

Badenburg

Opening times
Tue.–Sun. 10 a.m.–12.30 p.m. and 1.30–5 p.m.; closed in winter

The two-storey Badenburg, on the south side of the large lake (Grosser See), was built by Joseph Effner in 1719–21 as a bathing pavilion for Elector Max Emanuel.
The ground-plan is determined by the oval reception room, with rich stucco ornament (fruit and shells) and a ceiling-painting by J. Amigoni, "Apollo in the chariot of the Sun". The most notable feature of the vestibule (which also served as a games room) is its Chinese wallpaper with a pattern of birds, flowers and butterflies. The bedroom also has Chinese wallpaper, this time with life-size figures. The bathing room, which can claim to be Europe's first indoor swimming-pool, reaches down into the basement. The bath is faced with Dutch tiles; the walls of the gallery are decorated with prefabricated stucco-marble.
On the north side of the lake is the Temple of Apollo (Apollotempel), built for Ludwig I in 1865 to the design of Leo von Klenze. It contains a plan giving the dates of the different layouts of the park.

Magdalenenklause

Opening times
Tue.–Sun. 10 a.m.–12.30 p.m. and 1.30–5 p.m.; closed in winter

The Magdalenenklause (Magdalene Hermitage) was designed as a place of prayer and meditation for Elector Max Emanuel, but the Elector died before it was completed. The architect was Joseph Effner. It is a single-storey brick building with two apses, with artificially contrived cracks in the walls and crumbling plaster to give the effect of a ruin.
In the interior are a chapel and four cell-like rooms. The chapel, following the fashion of the period, is decorated with artificial corals and shells in the form of a grotto. The cells are panelled with stained oak.

Pagodenburg

The Pagodenburg, an elegant two-storey tea pavilion, was also built by Joseph Effner (1717–19). It was mainly used as a place for resting after pall-mall, a ball game played on a

Nymphenburg Palace: the central block and flanking pavilions

The Amalienburg

Nymphenburg Park

Opening times
Tue.–Sun. 10 a.m.–
12.30 p.m. and 1.30–5 p.m.;
closed in winter

horseshoe-shaped "mall" in the Pagodenburger Tal (valley) to the north.
The exterior is decorated with stucco masks (Bacchus, Flora, Neptune, Ceres), the interior in the then popular chinoiserie. On the ground floor is the "Salettl", with a ceiling-painting by G. Gumpp and walls faced with Dutch tiles. On the upper floor are three rooms. The Chinese Salon and Chinese Cabinet have panelling lacquered in black and red and silk wallpaper; the Rest Room is decorated in white, gold and green.

Odeonsplatz N18

U-Bahn
Odeonsplatz

The Odeonsplatz is the starting-point of Munich's first two great 19th c. monumental streets, the Brienner Strasse (see entry) and the Ludwigstrasse (see entry). Its rigorously neo-classical pattern was set between 1816 and 1828 by Leo von Klenze, who built the Leuchtenberg-Palais (see entry), the Basar (Bazaar) building on the Hofgarten side and the Odeon, a concert hall and ballroom which was destroyed in 1944.

*Oktoberfest (October Festival) O/P16

Location
Theresienwiese

U-Bahn
Goetheplatz

The Oktoberfest, the world's largest and most celebrated popular festival, is held every year at the end of September and beginning of October on the Theresienwiese. Work begins months in advance on the erection of the enormous marquees and other attractions which draw huge numbers of visitors, young and old, local people and incomers from far and wide – the great beer tents, cosy in spite of their size, the sideshows and other entertainments, the swings and roundabouts, the hair-raising switchbacks and giant wheels. The visitors make their jostling way along the broad, crowded avenues, enjoying the spectacle, the bright lights, the noise, the fun; trying their luck at the sideshows, having their hand read, buying anything that takes their fancy. Nor are creature comforts lacking. Beer, of course, takes first place, with its natural accompaniments, *hendl* (chicken) and *steckerlfische* (grilled fish). Each year new records are set in the consumption of beer and *hendl*. (The number of visitors is at present running at just under 6 million.)

S-Bahn
Hackerbrücke

Trams
14, 19, 20, 27

Bus
31

The Oktoberfest was celebrated for the first time in 1810 on the occasion of the marriage of the future King Ludwig I and Princess Therese of Saxony-Hildburghausen. The only attraction on that occasion was a horse-race. A cattle show was added in the following year; 1818 saw the first roundabouts and swings; and from 1820 onwards the attractions grew in number – sideshows, travelling shops, artistes of various kinds, anatomical curiosities.
In September 1980 a terrorist bomb killed twelve people (memorial at entrance).

Old Academy (Alte Akademie) 017

In the heart of the Pedestrian Zone (see entry), adjoining St Michael's Church (see entry), is the Old Academy, a large

Location
Neuhauser Strasse 51

The Oktoberfest in full swing

U-Bahn
Marienplatz

S-Bahn
Karlsplatz, Marienplatz

complex surrounding four courtyards which is now occupied by the Bavarian Statistical Office. This Renaissance building was erected between 1585 and 1597 for a Jesuit college and school (which had 1500 pupils). After the expulsion of the Jesuits in 1773 it housed the Court Library and Archives (1774–1885), a school of painting and sculpture (hence the name of Academy) and also, from 1826 to 1840, the University. It was destroyed during the Second World War but was rebuilt in 1954.
In front of the building is the Richard Strauss Fountain (Richard-Strauss-Brunnen), commemorating the greatest Munich-born composer. The 6 m (20 ft) high bronze column, with scenes from Strauss's opera "Salome", was the work of Hans Wimmer (1962).

Old Botanic Garden (Alter Botanischer Garten) N17

Location
Elisenstrasse

U-Bahn
Hauptbanhof

S-Bahn
Karlsplatz, Hauptbanhof

This park, which was the municipal Botanic Garden from 1814 to 1909, lies just north of the Old Law Courts (see entry) and the New Law Courts (see entry). Since it became a public park in 1935–37 it has provided an oasis of peace amid the rushing traffic of the city centre.
The gardens were originally laid out in 1808–14 by the landscape-gardener Ludwig von Sckell. The neo-classical gate on Lenbachplatz was erected in 1812 by Joseph Emanual Herigoyen. The Neptune Fountain (1935–37; photograph, p. 83) was the work of Joseph Wackerle.
A "Crystal Palace" was erected on the north side of the garden in 1854 for the first International Industrial Exhibition. This structure of steel and glass – progressive for its day – was destroyed by fire in 1931.

Old Law Courts (Alter Justizpalast) N/O17

Location
Elisenstrasse 1a

U-Bahn
Hauptbanhof

S-Bahn
Karlsplatz, Hauptbanhof

This monumental building with projecting side wings, in a mingling of Renaissance and Baroque, was erected by Friedrich von Thiersch between 1887 and 1897. The east end facing Karlsplatz (Stachus), with a vaulted middle section, has all the effect of a richly decorative main front. The four-sided dome over the central light well, constructed of steel and glass, was a novel feature at the time it was built.

*Old Town Hall (Altes Rathaus) O18

Location
Marienplatz 15

U-Bahn
Marienplatz

S-Bahn
Marienplatz

Munich's Gothic Town Hall, known since the 19th c. as the Old Town Hall, was built by Jörg von Halspach (known as Ganghofer) between 1470 and 1480. After undergoing modification in accordance with the taste of the day in the Late Renaissance and Baroque periods it was reconverted to the Gothic style in 1861–64. It was restored after the Second World War. The archway and passage for pedestrians date from the 19th c. Photograph, p. 85.
The 55 m (180 ft) high tower of the Old Town Hall, a prominent

Neptune Fountain, Old Botanic Garden ▶

feature at the east end of the Marienplatz, was rebuilt in 1975 after its destruction by wartime bombing.
The Council Chamber served also as the meeting-place of the Estates, a ballroom for patrician families, a dance-hall during the Shrovetide festivities and for civic receptions. It was also used by the Wittelsbach Dukes of Bavaria for state occasions.
The interior (not open to the public) is a masterpiece of medieval design. It has a barrel-vaulted timber roof with decorated beams and golden stars, a frieze of coats of arms (1478) and the celebrated figures of Morisco dancers by Erasmus Grasser (originals in Municipal Museum; see entry).

*Olympic Park (Olympiapark) J/K16

U-Bahn
Petuelring/Olympiazentrum

Buses
36, 41, 43, 81, 84, 136, 184

Conducted tours
11 a.m. and 2.30 p.m. in summer

The 20th Summer Olympic Games were held in Munich in 1972, and the necessary facilities were provided between 1967 and 1972 on an area of 2·7 million sq. m (667 acres) on the Oberwiesenfeld, which had previously been a military training ground and for a time a commercial airfield. The whole area was transformed into an attractive park fully equipped for sport and recreation, with the various facilities situated in a pleasant natural setting within convenient distances from each other.
The buildings required were designed to fit into the landscape – an objective largely achieved by the device of a long tent roof enclosing the main structures. There was much controversy over the high cost of all this, amounting in total to 1·35 billion DM, of which 522 million DM were accounted for by sports facilities and 92 million by landscaping.
The buildings were erected by a group of architects headed by Günther Behnisch. They include the Olympic Stadium (Olympiastadion), with seating for 78,000, used for major sporting events (football, track and field events); the Ice Stadium (Eissporthalle), with seating for 7000; the Olympic Hall (seating for 12,000), a multi-purpose hall which is used for sporting events, congresses, concerts and Shrovetide balls; the Swimming Hall (Schwimmhalle), with seating for 2000, which is now mainly used as an indoor swimming-pool; the Cycling Stadium (Radstadion), with seating for 5000; and the Volleyball Hall, with seating for 3700.
The tent roof, a daring technical achievement which is one of the sights of the Olympic Park, covers part of the Olympic Stadium, the Olympic Hall and the Swimming Hall. It consists of a network of cables (total length 436 km (271 miles)) and 8300 acrylic sheets suspended from 12 steel masts 50–80 m (165–260 ft) high set at an angle from the vertical. The 75,000 sq. m (90,000 sq. yd) of the roof can support loads of up to 5000 tonnes. The cost of the roof increased during the course of construction from 20 million DM to some 200 million.
The 290 m (950 ft) high television tower was built in 1965–68 and later renamed the Olympic Tower (Olympiaturm). It has two platforms, one containing telecommunications apparatus, the other a viewing platform at a height of 190 m (623 ft), which rotates on its axis, taking an hour to complete each revolution; this platform, with restaurants, affords breathtaking views of the city, the Alpine foreland and in good weather the mountains themselves.

Flower-stalls in front of the Old Town Hall ▶

In the north-east of the Olympic Park is the Olympic Village, consisting of a 14-storey block of flats opening off terraces (the former Men's Village) and the Studentstadt (Student City), with 800 two-storey houses and a 19-storey tower block (the former Women's Village).

The landscaping of the area included the creation of a lake 1200 m (1300 yd) long. On the north side of this Olympic Lake (Olympiasee) is the Theatron, in the form of an ancient (open-air) Greek theatre, periodically used for dramatic performances and every Sunday afternoon in summer for pop concerts. On the south side of the lake rises the Olympiaberg (Olympic Hill), built up after the last war of rubble from buildings destroyed by bombing. In preparation for the Olympics it was landscaped and laid out with footpaths.

Palaeontology and Geology Collection

See State Palaeontology and Geology Collection

Palais Porcia

N18

Location
Kardinal-Faulhaber-Strasse 12

U-Bahn
Odeonsplatz, Marienplatz

This Baroque palace, now occupied by the Bayerische Vereinsbank, was built by Enrico Zuccalli in 1693 for Count Fugger. Together with the Montgelas-Palais (see entry) and the Archbishop's Palace (see entry) it gives this part of the city its distinctive character. It was the first building in Munich modelled on the Italian palaces of the Baroque period. In 1731

The Olympic Stadium under its tent roof

Elector Charles Albert presented the palace to his mistress Countess Morawitzka, later Princess Porcia, and in 1736 François Cuvilliés remodelled it in Rococo style.

S-Bahn
Marienplatz

Pedestrian Zone (Fussgängerzone) O17–18/N18

After the completion of the U-Bahn and S-Bahn tunnel in the old town the municipal authorities resolved to limit the volume of traffic in the city centre by establishing an extensive pedestrian precinct in which people could walk about and do their shopping or window-shopping at leisure. In the centre of the zone is the Marienplatz, with the Old Town Hall (see entry), the New Town Hall (see entry). From there it extends westward along Kaufinger Strasse and Neuhauser Strasse to the Karlsplatz (see entry). In this section are a number of department stores belonging to the major chains. In Neuhauser Strasse are the Karlstor (see entry; Karlsplatz), Bürgersaal (see entry), Old Academy (see entry), St Michael's Church (see entry) and Hunting Museum (see entry). Near the Karlstor (at the Karstadt department store) is a popular figure, the Brunnenbuberl (Fountain Boy) by M. Gastinger (1895). To the north the pedestrian zone extends along Weinstrasse (to the left of the Town Hall) and Theatinerstrasse to the Odeonsplatz (see entry). In Theatinerstrasse, with its elegant and fashionable shops, are the Preysing-Palais (see entry) and Theatinerkirche (see entry).
Also within the pedestrian zone are the Frauenplatz (round the Frauenkirche; see entry) and some adjoining lanes, the

Location
Neuhauser Strasse,
Kaufinger Strasse,
Theatinerstrasse

U-Bahn
Marienplatz

S-Bahn
Marienplatz, Karlsplatz

In Munich's pedestrian zone, looking towards the Karlstor

Petersplatz (round St Peter's Church) and the Viktualienmarkt (see entry) in the southern part of the old town.
In good weather musicians, including many foreigners, play in the streets, a variety of dramatic performances are put on by amateur groups, and altogether the pedestrian zone becomes a kind of communication centre full of life and activity.

*Peterskirche

See St Peter's Church

Pippinger Kircherl

M9

Location
Pippinger Strasse 49a, Pipping

S-Bahn
Pasing

Buses
73, 76

The Pippinger Kircherl, officially the Church of St Wolfgang in Pipping, is a rare example of a Late Gothic village church which has survived without modification. Unusually for the Munich area, in which almost all the Gothic churches were remodelled in Baroque style, the interior of this church, built by Duke Sigismund in 1478–80, escaped the modernising zeal of the 16th and 17th c. The tower was rebuilt in 1794 with a steeple after being destroyed by lightening.
The wall-paintings in the chancel (Passion, Death of the Virgin, Prophets, Wise and Foolish Virgins) and the paintings of the Four Fathers of the Church on the stone pulpit were probably the work of Jan Polack (1479). The stained glass dates from 1478, the three carved altars (figure of St Wolfgang on High Altar) from 1490.

Prehistoric Collection

See State Prehistoric Collection

Preysing-Palais (Preysing Palace) N18

The Preysing-Palais, Munich's first Rococo palace, was built by Joseph Effner in 1723–28 for Count Maximilian von Preysing, Master of the Electoral Hunt. The Feldherrnhalle (see entry) was built against its north wall in 1841–44. During the Second World War it was so badly damaged that the outer walls, except the Residenzstrasse façade, had to be pulled down and rebuilt (1958–60). The interior, including the banqueting hall and chapel, had already been destroyed during the 19th c. and is now traversed by shopping arcades. The beautiful grand staircase with its caryatides has, however, survived.

Location
Residenzstrasse 27

U-Bahn
Odeonsplatz

*Prinz-Carl-Palais N18

This neo-classical palace, now the official residence of the Bavarian Prime Minister, was built by Karl von Fischer in 1804–06. It takes its name from Prince Carl, Ludwig I's brother, who occupied it from 1825 to 1875.
The façade, a model of classical proportion, is articulated by a

Location
Königinstrasse 1

U-Bahn
Odeonsplatz

Prinz-Carl-Palais, now the official residenz of the Bavarian Prime Minister

Buses
53, 55

series of colossal Ionic pilasters before which is a portico with a high pediment.
The palace originally stood in a park to the north of the Hofgarten. At the end of the 19th c. it acquired a new function in Munich's townscape as the terminal point of Prinzregentenstrasse at its western end.

Prinzregentenstrasse N19–O21

Buses
53, 55

Trams
18, 20

This was the last of Munich's great 19th c. streets to be constructed (1891–1912). It is named after Prince Regent Luitpold, who ruled Bavaria during the incapacity of Ludwig II and the insanity of King Otto. The street was laid out in accordance with the town-planning principles of the day, designed to secure a picturesque effect – with houses set back from the street, curves and sudden widenings so as to achieve variety and surprise. The Prinzregentenstrasse is in sharp contrast to the Ludwigstrasse (see entry), the dead straightness of which was considered dull by turn-of-the-century tastes.

*Propylaea (Propyläen) N17

Location
Königsplatz

U-Bahn
Königsplatz

This last genuinely classical structure in Munich was erected on the Königsplatz by Leo von Klenze in 1846–62. Modelled on the Propylaea on the Acropolis in Athens, its Doric style is in deliberate contrast to the Ionic Glyptothek (see entry) and the Corinthian State Collection of Antiquities (see entry). The sculpture in the pediment of the central portico glorifies the Greek struggle for independence from the Turks (1821–29); like the reliefs of scenes of combat on the flanking towers, it was the work of Ludwig Schwanthaler.

**Residence (Residenz) N/O18

Location
Max-Joseph-Platz 3

U-Bahn
Odeonsplatz

S-Bahn
Marienplatz

The Residence, for centuries the palace of the Dukes and Kings of Bavaria, occupies the site of a moated castle known as the Neuveste (New Stronghold) built at the end of the 14th c. to replace the Alter Hof (see entry), which had become too small and, after a popular rising in 1385, was felt to be insufficiently secure. The Neuveste reached its greatest extent about 1570; then in 1750 it was burned down, and was finally demolished in the 19th c. The present Residence, an extensive complex laid out round seven courtyards, is the result of six successive building phases:
1st phase, in the reign of Albert V (1550–79): the Antiquarium, the largest Renaissance hall north of the Alps (1569–71), set obliquely across the centre of the Residence.
2nd phase, in the reign of William V (1579–97): the ranges of Renaissance buildings between Residenzstrasse and the Antiquarium (Grottenhoftrakt, Erbprinzentrakt, Witwentrakt).
3rd phase, in the reign of Maximilian I (1598–1651): further work on the Renaissance ranges (*trompe-l'œil* architectural façade of this period), residential apartments round the Kaiserhof (Imperial Court).

Residenz: the Königsbau

Residenz: the Grotto Court (left) and Fountain Court, with the Wittelsbach Fountain

4th phase, in the reigns of Charles Albert (1726–45) and Maximilian III Joseph (1745–79): the Green Gallery range (south side), the Cuvilliés Theatre (see entry) or Old Residence Theatre (Altes Residenztheater).
5th phase, in the reign of Ludwig I (1825–48): enlargement of the palace to its present extent, with the National Theatre (see entry), the Königsbau (fronting on to Max-Joseph-Platz), the Festsaalbau (Banqueting Hall wing) on the north side (1835–42) and the north front of the building.
6th phase, after the Second World War: rebuilding after severe wartime destruction, store-rooms on the east side

Exterior

The predominant features of the exterior date from two different periods.
The neo-classical façade of the Königsbau on the south side of the complex (Max-Joseph-Platz), in the manner of the Renaissance palaces of Florence, and the façade of the

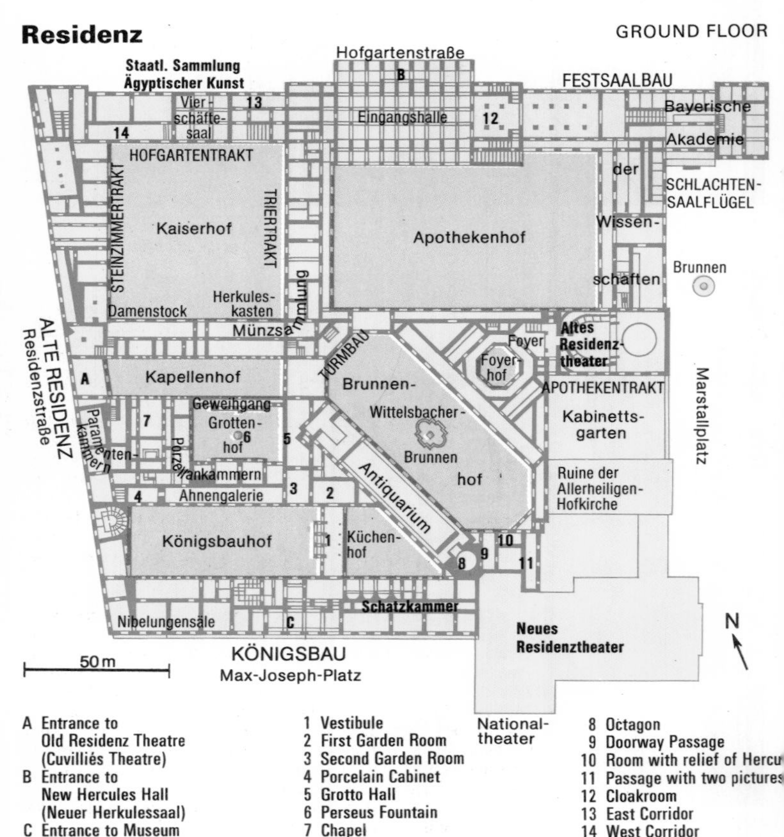

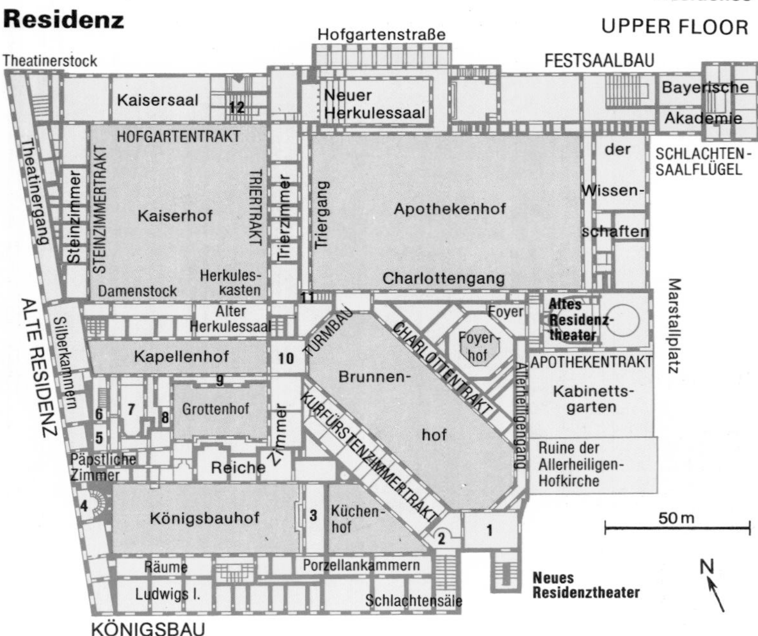

1 Black Hall
2 Yellow Staircase
3 Green Gallery
4 Queen Mother's Staircase
5 Chamber of Relics
6 Chapel Staircase
7 Court Chapel
8 Rich Chapel
9 Antler Corridor
10 St George's Hall
11 Broad Staircase
12 Imperial Staircase

Festsaalbau on the north side (Hofgartenstrasse) were built in the early 19th c.

The handsome west front was built at the beginning of the 17th c., with *trompe-l'œil* painting in tones of grey and blue to give the effect of architectural form and decoration. The two doorways, framed in red marble like triumphal arches, are surmounted by coats of arms and figures of the Virtues and guarded by bronze lions. In a niche in the centre of the façade is a bronze figure (by Hans Krumper, 1616) of Patrona Boiariae (Patroness of Bavaria) – the Virgin as Queen of Heaven with the Infant Jesus on a crescent moon.

Three of the seven courtyards (Kaiserhof, Kapellenhof, Brunnenhof) have *trompe-l'œil* painting like that on the west front. The narrow Kapellenhof (Chapel Court) was originally an old lane, the Jägergassl, which was incorporated in the Residence. The largest of the seven courtyards, the Apothekenhof (Pharmacy Court), is without decoration. For the Grottenhof and Königsbauhof, see under Residence Museum. The most handsome of the courtyards is the eight-sided Brunnenhof (Fountain Court), flanking the Antiquarium, which was built in 1610. In the centre of the courtyard is the large Wittelsbach Fountain (Wittelsbacher-Brunnen, 1611–23), erected in honour of Duke Otto. The bronze figure of the Duke is by Hans Krumper (1610–20), the reclining river

Residenz: the Antiquarium

gods (representing the Danube, the Isar, the Lech and the Inn), the standing figures of gods and goddesses (Ceres, Vulcan, Neptune, Juno) and the grotesque fishes, monsters, frogs and children by Hubert Gerhard and his pupils (*c.* 1600).
The rooms at the north-east corner of the Residence are occupied by the Bavarian Academy of Sciences (Bayerische Akademie der Wissenschaften).

**Residence Museum (Residenzmuseum) O18

Location
Max-Joseph-Platz 3

U-Bahn
Marienplatz, Odeonsplatz

S-Bahn
Marienplatz

Opening times
Tue.–Sat. 10 a.m.–4. 30 p.m., Sun. and pub. hol. 10 a.m.–1 p.m.

Conducted tours
Morning and afternoon

The last Bavarian King, Ludwig III, abdicated in 1918, and in 1920 his sumptuously decorated and furnished palace was opened to the public as a museum. The palace suffered heavy damage by bombing during the Second World War, but all movable furniture and furnishings had been removed to places of safety and survived. Some 60 million DM was spent on the restoration of the Residence between 1945 and 1980.
The Museum affords an excellent survey of the art of interior decoration from the 16th to the 19th c. and contains a celebrated collection of porcelain. Among features of particular interest are the following:
Gallery of Ancestors (Ahnengalerie): built by Joseph Effner (1726–31), decorated by Zimmermann, Dietrich and Miroffsky, with 212 portraits of Wittelsbach ancestors.
Porcelain Cabinet (Porzellankabinett): designed by Cuvilliés (1731–33); Nymphenburg, Frankenthal, Sèvres, Vienna, Meissen and Würzburg porcelain.
Grotto Court (Grottenhof): a Mannerist grotto constructed of

tufa, crystals and shells (1581–86), with a bronze figure of Mercury (probably by Giovanni da Bologna) and the Perseus Fountain by Hubert Gerhard (*c.* 1590).
Antiquarium: the first part of the present Residence to be built (by Egkl, 1569–71), a 69 m (226 ft) long hall with a barrel-vaulted roof and side vaults over the windows. Along the walls are antique busts and statues collected by Duke Albert V. Allegorical paintings on the vaulting by Peter Candid. In the window recesses are more than a hundred views of Bavarian towns and castles by Hans Donauer.
Battle Rooms (Schlachtensäle), with paintings of scenes from the Napoleonic Wars (1805–14); formerly antechambers to Ludwig I's apartments (Räume Ludwigs I.).
All Saints Corridor (Allerheiligengang; so called because it gave access to the Court Church of All Saints, the Allerheiligen-kirche, now ruined): cycle of frescoes on Italian travel (1830–33), painted by Carl Rottmann for the arcades of the Hofgarten or Kabinettgarten (Court Garden, Cabinet Garden).
Charlotte Rooms (Charlottenzimmer): named after Maximilian I Joseph's daughter, later wife of Emperor Francis I of Austria: characteristic examples of early 19th c. interior decoration.
Rich Apartments (Reiche Zimmer): a series of rooms round the Grotto Court; sumptuous Rococo interiors by Joseph Effner and François Cuvilliés (1726–37; restored).
Nibelung Rooms (Nibelungensäle): large frescoes of scenes from the "Nibelungenlied" by Schnorr von Carolsfeld, Olivier and Hauschil (1827–37, 1843–67).
Chamber of Relics (Reliquienkammer): a collection of valuable goldsmiths' work of the 16th–18th c. assembled by Maximilian I and his successors.
Rich Chapel (Reiche Kapelle): Maximilian I's private audience chamber, sumptuously decorated by Hans Krumper.
Silver Chambers (Silberkammern): 17th and 18th c. table silver from German and French workshops; the Wittelsbach table silver (3500 items).
Stone Rooms (Steinzimmer): named after the stucco-marble decoration (1612–17), reflecting Maximilian I's conception of the world; sumptuous furnishings (sculpture, furniture, 17th c. tapestries).

Treasury (Schatzkammer)

Opening times
Tue.–Sat. 10 a.m.–4.30 p.m., Sun. and pub. hol. 10 a.m.–1 p.m.

The treasures assembled by Dukes and Electors over the centuries make this one of the largest, most important and most valuable collections of the kind. The Treasury was founded by Duke Albert V (1550–79) with the "house jewels" of the Wittelsbachs, the ownership of which could not be transferred to another family. In the reign of Charles Theodore (1777–79) further treasures came from Heidelberg, Düsseldorf and Mannheim. The latest items in the collection are the insignia of the kingdom of Bavaria established in 1806.
Arrangement of the rooms:
Room I: early and late Middle Ages; Emperor Charles the Bald's prayer-book (*c.* 860), crown of Empress Kunigunde, reliquary of True Cross which belonged to the Emperor Henry II and cross which belonged to Queen Gisela (all *c.* 1000), English Queen's crown (*c.* 1370).
Room II: Late Gothic and Early Renaissance; ostrich-egg ciborium (*c.* 1440), Rappoltsheim Goblet (*c.* 1540).

Room III: statuette of St George (*c.* 1599) from Munich.
Room IV: religious art of the Renaissance and Baroque periods; domestic altar of Albert V (*c.* 1560), domestic altar from southern Germany (*c.* 1580), Augsburg Crucifix (by G. Petel, *c.* 1630).
Room V: insignia and orders of the Bavarian kings, including insignia of the Emperor Charles VII, ceremonial sword and ruby jewellery which belonged to Queen Therese (*c.* 1830).
Rooms VI and VII: cut gems and rock-crystal (second half of 16th c.).
Room VIII: High and Late Renaissance; goldsmiths' work and amber articles, including fine goblets and ornamental vessels.
Room IX: Baroque and Rococo; goldsmiths' work, tableware, toilet sets.
Room X: non-European arts and crafts, including ivory carvings from Ceylon, Turkish daggers and Chinese porcelain.

* Residence Theatre, New

See Theatre: Bavarian State

** Residence Theatre, Old

See Cuvilliés Theatre

St Anne's Church (Damenstiftskirche St Anna) O17

Location
Damenstiftstrasse 1

U-Bahn
Marienplatz,
Sendlinger-Tor-Platz

S-Bahn
Karlsplatz, Marienplatz

St Anne's Church, once attached to a convent for a gentlewomen which is now a girls' secondary school, was built by Johann Baptist Gunetzrhainer in 1732–35. During the Second World War it was destroyed by bombing, leaving only the outer walls and the façade, but was rebuilt in its original form in the 1950s.
The façade, with a wide middle section flanked by narrower lateral sections, is broken up by pilasters on tall bases. It survived the war unscathed.
The interior, consisting of a porch (with gallery), a square nave, short transepts and a rectangular chancel, is divided into bays by wide arches and roofed with shallow domes. It is attractively decorated in pink, blue, white and gold.
The altars have been reconstructed, incorporating figures which survived the bombing. The High Altar has a painting by Joseph Ruffini of the Virgin and Child with St Anne; in front is a "Last Supper" with over-life-size figures (18th c.). On the right-hand side altar is a painting by Balthasar Augustin Albrecht, "Glorification of St François de Sales", on the left-hand side altar a "Visitation" by Georges Desmarées. The stucco-work by Egid Quirin Asam has been restored; the frescoes, in tones of grey, by his brother Cosmas Damian have been repainted ("Homage of the Angels" in chancel, "Glorification of St Anne and the Virgin" in nave, "Angels' Concert" in porch).
In Damenstiftstrasse are two handsome secular buildings – at No. 4 a house in neo-classical style (*c.* 1800) and at No. 8 the Rococo Palais Lerchenfeld (by A. Gunetzrhainer, 1726).

St Anne's Church: ceiling fresco and Bavarian coat of arms

*St Anne's Church (Sankt-Anna-Klosterkirche) N/O19

Location
Sankt-Anna-Platz

S-Bahn
Isartor

Trams
14, 19, 20

The Monastic Church of St Anne, built by Johann Michael Fischer in 1727–33, was the first Rococo church in Old Bavaria (i.e. Bavaria within its smaller pre-1803 boundaries). Its central plan was a novelty: the Italian pattern of a rectilinear nave with pilasters now gave place to a central oval with niches and with the chancel and porch built on at either end.

The church was badly damaged during the Second World War, and the reconstruction of the building, decoration and furnishings took many years. In the course of this work the church's beautiful Rococo façade (concealed since 1853 by a neo-Romanesque façade built on to it) was brought to light and restored.

The fine interior decoration and furnishings (largely reconstructed) were the work of the Asam brothers and Johann Baptist Straub.

High Altar: tabernacle and angels in adoration by Straub (1737); stucco figures by Egid Quirin Asam; altar-piece by Asam (reconstructed), "St Anne teaching Mary the Scriptures in the presence of St Joachim".

Front niches: altar-pieces, "The last Communion of St Jerome" (right) and "St Paula of Rome with her daughter Eustachia" (left).

Side niches: Early Baroque figure of St Anthony (1682; right), altar with 17th c. "Mater Dolorosa" (left).

Frescoes: scenes from the life of St Anne (by Asam, reconstructed).

St Boniface's Church (Bonifatiusbasilika) N17

Location
Karlstrasse 34

U-Bahn
Königsplatz

S-Bahn
Hauptbahnhof

The Benedictine Monastic Church of St Boniface, which is also the parish church of the Maxvorstadt, was built in 1834–47 in Byzantine style to the designs of Georg Friedrich Ziebland. After its destruction during the Second World War Hans Döllgast rebuilt the south end and porch, and later a modern conventual building was constructed on the ruins of the north end and the apse. In the aisle on the east side (to the right of the main entrance) is the tomb of King Ludwig I.

The old conventual buildings originally linked the building which now houses the State Collection of Antiquities (see entry) with the apse of the church – a bringing together of religion (the Church), learning (the monastery) and art (the museum) which appealed to the Romantic educational ideal of the first half of the 19th c.

St George's Church (Sankt Georg) N20

Location
Bogenhausener Kirchplatz 1, Bogenhausen

Bus
54

Tram
20

This little Rococo church, picturesquely situated in a village churchyard, was built by Johann Michael Fischer in 1766–68. The choir, however, is Late Gothic – a survival from an earlier, originally Romanesque, church.

The theatrical High Altar, with figures of St George on Horseback, St Donatus and St Irene, was the work of Johann Baptist Straub. The right-hand side altar, with a figure of St Corbinian (in the centre), and the pulpit are by Ignaz Günther;

The little Rococo Church of St George in Bogenhausen

the left-hand side altar, with a Virgin enthroned (*c.* 1628) is by unknown artists. There are notable ceiling-paintings in the chancel and the east end of the nave (by Helterhof, 1770), "St George received in heaven" and "Martyrdom of St George".

St Mary's Church (Sankt Maria)

Q21

This little church is one of the oldest pilgrimage churches in Old Bavaria. The present Late Gothic building, on the site of an earlier 11th c. church, was erected in 1399 and remodelled in Baroque style in 1675. The Gothic tower was topped with a dome in 1792. The image of the Virgin on the High Altar dates from about 1480 and may have been the work of Erasmus Grasser. Also of the Late Gothic period is the winged altar on the north wall of the nave, with a high relief of the Crucifixion by Grasser (1483). The panel-painting of the Virgin of Mercy (Schutzmantelmadonna) on the south wall dates from 1503.

Location
Aribonenstrasse 9, Ramersdorf

U-Bahn
Karl-Preis-Platz

Buses
95, 96

St Matthew's Church (Matthäuskirche)

O17

St Matthew's Church, an Evangelical (Protestant) cathedral, stands in a dominant position in Sendlinger-Tor-Platz. Built in 1953–55 to the design of G. Gsaenger, it is an unconventional structure on a curving plan with a curved roof which has become irreverently known as "God's bath-tub". The plain square tower is in sharp contrast to the church.
The interior, with its six tall columns supporting the roof, is of impressive effect. On the chancel wall is a marble mosaic by A. Gsaenger, symbolising – in a fashion characteristic of post-war religious art – sorrow, guilt and death. The huge Crucifix over the altar is by R. Schwarzkopf.
As one of the first modern churches to be built in Munich, St Matthew's served as a model, pointing the way forward for other new churches.

Location
Nussbaumstrasse 1

U-Bahn
Sendlinger-Tor-Platz

**St Michael's Church (Michaelskirche)

O18

St Michael's, the largest Renaissance church north of the Alps, was built by Duke William the Pious in 1583–97 as a spiritual centre of the Counter-Reformation. It was erected in two stages. In the first stage (1583–88) the church was built and given a barrel-vaulted roof by an unknown architect (the vault being the largest in the world apart from that of St Peter's in Rome). There were grave doubts about the stability of the vaulting; but in fact it was the tower that collapsed and destroyed the choir in 1590. Thereupon, in a second building phase lasting until 1597, Friedrich Sustris built on to the undamaged nave a new choir and a transept which had not been provided for in the original plan. After suffering severe damage during the Second World War the church was rebuilt in 1946–48. Further restoration work was completed in 1983.

Location
Neuhauser Strasse 52

U-Bahn
Marienplatz

S-Bahn
Karlsplatz

Opening times
Ducal burial-vault: spring to 2 Nov., Mon.–Fri. 10 a.m.–1 p.m. and 3–4.45 p.m., Sat. 10 a.m.–3 p.m.

Façade

With the Old Academy (see entry) and the former Augustinian church now occupied by the Hunting Museum (see entry), St

St Michael's Church: the façade

The imposing interior of St Michael's Church

Michael's Church forms an impressive ensemble. Its façade is a masterpiece of proportion. Divided horizontally by three bold cornices, it is given a character of unity by its windows, doorways and niches, which are all round-headed.
The figures on the façade present the political programme of the Counter-Reformation. In the ground-floor niche the Archangel Michael (a magnificent bronze figure by Hubert Gerhard, 1588) is depicted fighting evil in the world, while in the smaller niches on the upper levels are stone figures (by unknown sculptors) of the kings and dukes who spread Christianity in Bavaria.

Interior

The aisleless nave with its high barrel-vaulted roof is of impressive spatial effect. The dominant feature is the triumphal arch at the entrance to the choir, the pattern of which is continued in the arches of the transepts, side chapels and galleries.
The furnishing of the interior with altars and figures is dictated by a rigorous programme of atonement and purification. A striking feature is the tall three-storey High Altar, a joint work by Sustris, Wendel Dietrich and Christoph Schwarz; the altar-piece, "St Michael fighting the Devil" (1587) is by Schwarz. The four bronze reliefs by Gerhard (*c.* 1595) were intended for the tomb which Duke William V wanted to have erected under the triumphal arch but which was never executed. In the side chapels are good pictures by Peter Candid, Hans von Aachen and Antonio Viviani and a precious reliquary of SS. Cosmas and Damian (*c.* 1400, Bremen).

*St Michael's Church (Sankt Michael), Berg am Laim — P22

Location
Clemens-August-Strasse 9, Berg am Laim

U-Bahn
Michaelibad

Tram
14

St Michael's Church in Berg am Laim, one of the most perfect Rococo churches in Bavaria and the most beautiful church in eastern Munich, was built by Johann Michael Fischer in 1738-58 for Archbishop Clemens August of Cologne, son of Elector Maximilian Emanuel, who held the nearby castle of Berg am Laim. This former court church, which was served by a Brotherhood of St Michael, has been since 1913 the parish church of Baumkirchen ward.
The handsome façade, with its twin towers forming a strong vertical accent, was designed as the terminal feature of a street which was never built. The central section is flanked by double columns. Over the main doorway is a shallow niche containing a figure of St Michael (1911) which appears unduly small for its setting.
The interior of the church is dominated by the large round-headed arches between the different sections. The rectangular central space is articulated by pilasters and columns and the corners are rounded off by niches. The beautiful ceiling paintings (episodes from the life of St Michael) are by Johann Baptist Zimmermann, the high altar and the altars in the central area by Johann Baptist Straub. The gilded figures on either side of the tabernacle are attributed to Ignaz Günther.

*St Peter's Church (Peterskirche) O18

Location
Rindermarkt 1

U-Bahn
Marienplatz

S-Bahn
Marienplatz

Opening times
Tower: Mon.–Sat. 9 a.m.–4 p.m., Sun. and pub. hol. 10 a.m.–4 p.m.

St Peter's Church, Munich's oldest parish church and for long its only one, stands on the Petersbergl, a slight eminence which was occupied by monks before the foundation of the town.
The church has a complicated history. It was preceded by an 11th c. Romanesque basilica (first mentioned in the records in 1169) which was destroyed in a great fire in 1327. The present church was built in Gothic style in 1379–86 but was subsequently altered by the addition of a Baroque choir with three apses in 1630–36, the substitution of a barrel-vaulted roof and the remodelling of the interior in Baroque style (1651–54). Between 1607 and 1621 the tower – known as Alter Peter (Old Peter) – was given a lantern dome in place of its earlier Gothic spire.
Notable features of the interior are the font by Hans Krumper (under the tower), red marble monuments by Erasmus Grasser (set into the west wall,) the Schrenk Altar (north aisle), with sculptures of the Crucifixion and the Last Judgment, and the High Altar, 20 m (65 ft) in height. The High Altar (by N. Stuber, 1730) has figures (by E. Q. Asam) of the Four Fathers of the Church and a figure of St Peter by Erasmus Grasser from an altar of 1517. The panel-paintings on the choir walls are by Jan Polack.

St Salvator's Church (Salvatorkirche) N18

Location
Salvatorplatz 17

U-Bahn
Odeonsplatz

This brick-built Late Gothic church with its tall steeple was built by Lukas Rottaler in 1493–94. Originally the cemetery church of the parish of Our Lady, it is now the church of Munich's Greek Orthodox community. The churchyard, which was closed in 1789, contains the graves of Orlando di Lasso and François Cuvilliés. There are remains of Gothic frescoes in the Ridler Memorial Chapel on the north side of the church.

*Schack Gallery (Schackgalerie) N19

Location
Prinzregentenstrasse 9

Buses
53, 55

Tram
20

Opening times
Daily except Tue. 9 a.m.–4.30 p.m.

The Schack Gallery has a notable collection illustrating the development of German painting in the 19th c. Its founder, Count Adolf Friedrich von Schack (1815–94), was a generous art patron, buying and commissioning works by many 19th c. German painters, including Schwind, Spitzweg, Lenbach and Böcklin. His collection, which he bequeathed to the German Emperor, now forms part of the Bavarian State collections.
The collection is divided into three sections.
Ground floor: the Early Romantic school and their successors (Koch, Dillis, Schnorr von Carolsfeld, Schwind, Neureuther, Spitzweg, etc.).
First floor: Idealist painting (Böcklin, Feuerbach, Marées, Lenbach, Piloty, etc.).
Second floor: post-Romantic schools (Kraus, Bode, Morgenstern, Hagn, A. E. Kirchner, etc.).

Side chapels in St Peter's Church

Schäftlarn Abbey (Kloster Schäftlarn)

About the year 760 Benedictine monks settled in the Isar Valley and founded Schäftlarn Abbey, only to abandon it in the 10th c. About 1140 it was rebuilt and granted by the Bishop of Freising to Premonstratensian Canons.
The abbey as we see it today dates from the 18th c. The monastic buildings (1702–06) were designed by Viscardi; the church was begun by Cuvilliés in 1733 and completed by Gunetzrhainer, on a simpler plan, in 1751–57. The frescoes and stucco-work are by J. B. Zimmermann, the altars and pulpit by J. B. Straub.

Location
Schäftlarn

S-Bahn
Ebenhausen-Schäftlarn

Distance
20 km (12½ miles) S

*Schleissheim

Schleissheim, on the eastern edge of the Dachauer Moos (Dachau Moss), is famous for its three handsome palaces.
Duke William V retired to Schleissheim to devote himself to religious contemplation. Here he purchased isolated farm-houses, erected hermitages and chapels and built himself a modest country house. His son, Elector Maximilian I, completed the house now known as the Old Palace.

Distance
13 km (8 miles) N

S-Bahn
Oberschleissheim

Bus
292

Schleissheim Old Palace

The Old Palace is an unpretentious manor house with two corner turrets and a flight of steps leading up to entrance, built

Location
Max-Emmanuel-Platz

by Heinrich Schön the Elder in 1616–23. Badly damaged by fire in 1944, the exterior was restored after the war (work completed 1972). Behind the house is a courtyard with old trees, from which a gatehouse gives access to the domestic offices of William V's original house.
The Old Palace lies opposite the New Palace, and under the original plan, which was not carried out, was to be incorporated with it in a four-square layout surrounding a central courtyard.

Schleissheim New Palace

Opening times
Tue.–Sun. 10 a.m.–12.30 p.m. and 1.30–5 p.m.

After his victory over the Turks in 1688 Duke Maximilian Emanuel returned in triumph to Munich and gave orders for the construction of a large new palace at Schleissheim to glorify his military exploits and display his power.
Although the original plan for an immense palace of four wings laid out round a courtyard had to be abandoned and only the east wing was actually built, Schleissheim New Palace is still one of the largest Baroque palaces in Germany. The architects were Enrico Zuccalli (1701–04) and Joseph Effner (1719–27).
Compared with its great length, the palace is of relatively modest height and depth. The central block, one storey higher, is given additional distinction by its colossal pilasters and large round-headed windows. Garden pavilions flanking the main building and linked with it by arcades increase still further the enormous length of the structure. The fine carving on the main doors of both fronts was the work of Ignaz Günther.
The particular charm of the beautifully designed and decorated interior lies in the mingling of Italian Late Baroque and Early Rococo.
The following rooms are particularly fine:
Entrance Hall, with eight red marble columns and *trompe-l'œil* paintings by Nikolaus Stuber in the low domes framed in stucco ornament.
Garden Room, with grisaille paintings by Stuber and stucco-work (sea monsters) by Giuseppe Volpini.
Staircase Hall, with green marble columns and Corinthian pilasters; stucco ornament (Turkish trophies) over the windows and doors, alluding to the victory over the Turks; fresco in dome, "Vulcan and Venus", by Cosmas Damian Asam.
Great Hall, with stucco ornament by Johann Baptist Zimmermann and two huge battle pictures ("Battle of Mohács" and "Relief of Vienna") by Franz Joachim Beich; ceiling-painting, "Aeneas and Turnus fighting for Princess Lavinia", by Jacopo Amigoni.
Hall of Victories, with battle pictures by Beich and a fresco by Amigoni, "Dido greeting Aeneas". Formerly the dining-room, this ranks among the finest of Baroque rooms.
Great Gallery: a Baroque gallery 61 m (200 ft) long, originally designed to house Maximilian Emanuel's collection of pictures, which are now in the Alte Pinakothek (see entry); they have been replaced by Dutch, Flemish and Italian works of the 17th and 18th c.

Schleissheim Baroque Gardens

Between the New Palace and the garden palace of Lustheim, covering an area 1250 m (1370 yd) by 350 m (380 yd), is one of the few Baroque gardens in Germany which has survived in

Schleissheim New Palace, one of the largest Baroque palaces in Germany

its original state. The eastern half was laid out in 1684; then in 1720–24 the gardens was extended and altered by Effner and D. Girard. In front of the New Palace is a parterre, with a fountain and cascade (1724); beyond this are two square gardens enclosed by hedges; and beyond these again, in the centre of the park, is a round central garden.

Lustheim Palace

This little garden palace in the Italian style was built by Enrico Zuccalli on the occasion of the marriage of Maximilian Emanuel with Maria Antonia, daughter of Emperor Leopold I of Austria. It consists of a central block, topped by a belvedere, and two side wings.

On the ground and lower ground floors is displayed Ernst Schneider's superb collection of Meissen porcelain, installed here in 1971. There are more than 1800 items, arranged chronologically and thermatically, ranging in date from 1710, when the Meissen manufactory was established, to the Seven Years War (1756–63). The collection includes Johann Friedrich Böttger's first experiments with stoneware as well as the costly dinner-services with animal designs which were supplied to the courts of Europe.

Location
Hochmuttinger Strasse

Opening times
Tue.–Sun. 10 a.m.–
12.30 p.m. and 1.30–5 p.m.
(in winter to 4 p.m.)

Schwabing

L/M18/19

The district of Schwabing begins just north of the Siegestor (see entry).

The name "Swapinga" first appears in the records in 782, long

S-Bahn
Münchner Freiheit,
Giselastrasse

The Siegestor, with Bavaria in her chariot

before the foundation of Munich. At the beginning of the 19th c. Schwabing was still a mere village with little more than 500 inhabitants, but it began to develop after the construction of the Ludwigstrasse (see entry), which linked it with Munich. In 1887 it acquired its municipal charter, but only four years later, in 1891, was incorporated in Munich.

Its fame as the artists' quarter of Munich began at the turn of the century, when painters, writers, poets, musicians and actors settled here, leading the *vie de bohème* in studios, artists' bars and the Englischer Garten. The good citizens of Munich tended to regard them as layabouts, though many artists and writers who were by no means layabouts also lived in Schwabing, including Joachim Ringelnatz, Franz Wedekind and Thomas Mann.

Unfortunately Schwabing is now steadily losing its distinctive character. Few of the artists' old haunts are left, rents have soared to astronomical heights and houses in Schwabing sell for record sums: it has become an "in" place to live.

*Siegestor (Victory Gate) M18

U-Bahn
Universität, Giselastrasse

This triumphal arch, modelled on the Arch of Constantine in Rome, was built by Friedrich von Gärtner in 1843–52 as the terminal point of the Ludwigstrasse (see entry). It commemorates the valour of the Bavarian Army, thus forming a counterpart to the Feldherrnhalle at the south end of the Ludwigstrasse, which honours Bavarian generals.

The Siegestor was badly damaged during the Second World

War and was not fully restored. Its new inscription (1958) reads: "Dedicated to victory, destroyed by war, calling for peace." The arch is topped by a figure of Bavaria in a chariot drawn by lions.

Siemens Museum

This museum illustrates – with original apparatus, models, displays and documents – the advance of electrical technology from its beginnings to the forward-looking developments of the present day, with particular reference to the contribution made by the firm of Siemens. The generation of power, land transport, communications technology, computers and semi-conductors, with their interfaces and peripheral developments, are but a few of the fields covered by this very instructive museum. There is also a section devoted to the history of Siemens. For those who want to pursue the matter further there are lectures by experts in various fields as well as film presentations.

Location
Prannerstrasse 10

U-Bahn
Odeonsplatz, Marienplatz

S-Bahn
Marienplatz

Opening times
Mon.–Fri. 9 a.m.–4 p.m., Sat. and Sun. 10 a.m.–2 p.m.

Southern Cemetery (Südfriedhof)

P17

The Southern Cemetery – since 1944 a public park – was the burial-place of many notable 18th and 19th c. figures. It was established in 1563, well outside the city walls, for the burial of the poor; in the 17th c. it was used for the burial of plague victims; and after the closure of other burial-places in the town centre it became Munich's principal cemetery. In 1844 an additional area was taken in on the south side of the cemetery, surrounded with arcades on the model of the Campo Santo in Bologna.
A visit to this cemetery is a novel way of learning something of the history of Munich and of Bavaria.

Location
Thalkirchner Strasse 17

S-Bahn
Sendlinger-Tor-Platz

Stachus (Karlsplatz)

O17

The Karlsplatz, outside the Karlstor, was laid out in 1791 after the demolition of the old town walls. It is named after the unpopular Elector Charles Theodore, but is familiarly known to the people of Munich as Stachus – a name whose origin has not been certainly established.
As a result of the development of the Altstadtring (the ring of boulevards round the old town) the Karlsplatz lost its original layout and gained the doubtful distinction of being one of the busiest traffic intersections in Europe. The buildings surrounding the square, originally erected about 1800, were given an additional storey and uniform façades by Gabriel von Seidl about 1900.
Below ground-level is the Stachus shopping centre (completed in 1970 at a cost of 173 million DM), with large numbers of shops, a pedestrian precinct and passages giving access to tram stops and the S-Bahn station.
At the end of Neuhauser Strasse is the Karlstor (previously known as the Neuhauser Tor), which formed part of the town's

S-Bahn
Karlsplatz

Stachus, one of Europe's busiest squares

second circuit of walls (14th c.); it was given its present name, after Elector Charles Theodore, in 1791. The main tower (1302) was demolished in 1857 after an explosion.

*Starnberger See

S-Bahn
Starnberg, Possenhofen, Feldafing, Tutzing

Distance
28 km (17 miles) SW

The Starnberger See, the second largest lake in Upper Bavaria (20 km ($12\frac{1}{2}$ miles) long, 2–5 km ($1\frac{1}{4}$–3 miles) across, greatest depth 123 m (404 ft)), occupies a depression gouged out by an Ice Age glacier, in an attractive setting of wooded hills dotted with castles, country houses and little towns and villages. It offers a beautiful scene on a fine summer day, when the chain of the Alps can be seen to the south, the waters of the lake are spangled with sailing-boats and wind-surfers, and the lake steamers go about their business. The lake is, however, notorious for the storms which can blow up without warning (visitors should watch out for the flashing lights).

At the north end of the lake is the little town of Starnberg (pop. 17,000), which has a popular lakeside promenade and a 16th c. castle (originally founded in the Middle Ages) high above the town. The Old Parish Church (1764–66) has a Late Rococo pulpit and High Altar by Ignaz Günther.

There are numbers of beautiful beaches on the shores of the lake, and many popular holiday villages (Possenhofen, Tutzing, Bernried, Seeshaupt, Leoni, Ammerland, etc.).

State Anthropological Collection (Anthropologische Staatssammlung) N17

This collection contains material illustrating the origin and development of man – skeletons and models of the lower apes, anthropoid apes and Stone Age types of early man. Particularly important items are the Palaeolithic *Homo sapiens sapiens* from the Klausenhöhle (cave) in the Altmühl Valley and the skulls and skeletons from the Ofnet Cave near Nördlingen.

Location
Karolinenplatz 2a

U-Bahn
Königsplatz

Not open to public

State Coin Collection (Staatliche Münzsammlung) O18

The State Coin Collection was established by Duke Albert V in 1570 and has been continuously added to, until it is now one of the largest collections of the kind in the world. It offers an excellent survey of money from Greek and Roman times down to the present day. It can display only a selection of its riches, including valuable medals, gems and cameos as well as coins.

Location
Residenzstrasse 1

U-Bahn
Odeonsplatz

Opening times
Tue.–Sun. 10 a.m.–5 p.m.

*State Collection of Antiquities (Staatliche Antikensammlungen) N17

The State Collection of Antiquities is housed in a building in late neo-classical style (by Georg Friedrich Ziebland, 1838–48) opposite the Glyptothek (see entry). The building was originally occupied by an "Exhibition of Art and Industry"; in 1898 it became the Haus der Secession (the name given to a group of avante-garde artists), and in 1919 the New State Gallery. After suffering severe damage during the Second World War it was restored in 1962–66 to house the Collection of Antiquities.

The collection comprises a magnificent array of vases, together with small artefacts, pottery, terracottas, small bronzes, glass and gold jewellery.

Particularly fine and valuable items include:
The Helicon Lekythos (Room I, case D).
The Dionysus Dish (Room II, case 12).
The amphora of Andodices (Room III, case 6).
Roman reticulated glass (Room VIII, case 2).
A Greek bronze, the "Maiden of Beroea" (Room VIII, case 3).
A Spartan standing mirror (Room IX, case 1).
A gold funerary garland from Armento (Room X, case 2).

Location
Königsplatz 1

U-Bahn
Königsplatz

Opening times
Tue., Thu. and Sun.
10 a.m.–4.30 p.m., Wed.
midday–8.30 p.m.

Conducted tours
Wed. 7 p.m.

**State Gallery of Modern Art (Straatsgalerie moderner Kunst) N19

The State Gallery of Modern Art is in the Haus der Kunst (House of Art), the first great show building of the Nazi period in Munich (by Paul Ludwig Troost, 1933–37), replacing the Crystal Palace, which had been burned down in 1931 (Botanic Gardens: see entry). Along the front of this squat and massive building runs a seemingly endless row of columns with no structural function.

The east wing and central section of the Haus der Kunst are used for special exhibitions, including the Great Art Exhibition

Location
Prinzregentenstrasse 1

U-Bahn
Odeonsplatz

Buses
53, 55

The Haus der Kunst, a showpiece of Nazi architecture

Opening times
Tue.–Sun. 9 a.m.–4.30 p.m.
(also 7–9 p.m. on Thu.)

(Grosse Kunstausstellung), held annually in autumn, for the display and sale of works by Munich artists. The State Gallery of Modern Art occupies the west wing.
The Gallery is devoted to 20th c. works of painting and sculpture by artists of many nations. During the Nazi period many works of art were destroyed by the authorities as "degenerate", including works by Van Gogh, Kokoschka, Munch and Nolde.
All the significant schools of the 20th c. are represented – the Fauves and early Expressionists (Matisse, Braque, Picasso, Munch), the Brücke group (E. L. Kirchner, Heckel, Mueller, Nolde, Schmidt-Rottluff), the Cubists (Picasso, Braque, Léger, Delaunay, Chagall), the Blauer Reiter group (Marc, Kandinsky, Corinth, Kokoschka), the Surrealists (de Chirico, Dali, Miró, Klee; Theo Wormland Collection), the Bauhaus, the Neue Sachlichkeit (New Functionalism) movement, abstract painting from 1930 to the present day (R. Motherwell, etc.), Minimal Art, Op Art, Pop Art.

*State Library (Staatsbibliothek) N18

Location
Ludwigstrasse 16

U-Bahn
University

The Bavarian State Library is Munich's largest library, with some 4·8 million volumes and manuscripts.
This long range of buildings, with seven wings laid out two courtyards, was built by Friedrich von Gärtner in 1834–39 within the plan for the development of the Ludwigstrasse (see entry). The style is modelled on that of the Early Renaissance palaces of Italy. The strong emphasis on the horizontal

articulation of the façade contributes to the continuity and monumental effect of the street.

Opening times
Main reading room:
Mon.–Fri. 9 a.m.–8 p.m.,
Sat. 9 a.m.–5 p.m.

*State Museum of Ethnology (Staatliches Museum für Völkerkunde) O19

The State Museum of Ethnology has large collections of art and artefacts from all over the world with the exception of Europe. It started as a collection of curios assembled by the Dukes and Electors of Bavaria and thereafter was continually added to. The most valuable part of the museum is the Preetorius Collection with its magnificent works of art from the East.
Asia: Chinese art, East Asian lacquerware, Buddhist art, Islamic weapons and booty from the Turkish Wars; Preetorius Collection (art of the East).
America: Mexico and Peru (ancient textiles, pottery, masks, figures and jewellery), Alaska (skins, implements), the North-West (Indian wigwams, masks, paintings).
Africa: West Africa (masks, sculpture, weapons); Ethiopia (silver jewellery and ornaments); Benin and Upper Guinea (ivory carvings, bronzes); East and South Africa (ornaments and jewellery).

Location
Maximilianstrasse 42

Bus
53

Trams
14, 19

Opening times
Tue.–Sun. 9.30 a.m.–4.30 p.m.

State Palaeontology and Geology Collection
(Staatliche Sammlung Paläontologie und historische Geologie) N17

The palaeontological section of this collection displays a wide range of fossils, including saurians, mammals (skeleton of a primitive form of elephant) and plants. The specimens come from all over the world, but the particular strength of the collection lies in the material from the Jurassic hills of Franconia and Swabia. The geological section is notable for the material illustrating the stratification of rocks in the Eastern Alps and Bavaria (Nördlinger Ries meteorite crater).

Location
Richard-Wagner-Strasse 10

U-Bahn
Königsplatz

Opening times
Mon.–Thu. 8 a.m.–4 p.m.,
Fri. 8 a.m.–3 p.m.

State Prehistoric Collection (Prähistorische Staatssammlung) N19

This collection was founded by the anthropologist Johannes Ranke in 1895, and since then archaeological material from Bavaria and the Mediterranean area has been collected and recorded here. The collections extend in time from the emergence of *Homo sapiens* by way of the Celtic settlement and the Roman period to the dawn of modern times.
The prehistoric section is on the upper floor: Stone Age in Room 1, Bronze Age, Urnfield culture and Hallstatt period in Rooms 2–4, Celtic period in Rooms 5 and 6.
The Roman section on the lower floor includes frescoes and mosaics and material on the Roman Conquest and the consolidation of Roman power (Room 7), the flowering of Roman civilisation (Room 8) and the late period and the end of Roman rule.

Location
Lerchenfeldstrasse 2

Buses
53, 55

Tram
20

Opening times
Tue.–Sun. 9.30 a.m.–4 p.m.,
Thu. to 8 p.m.

Villa Stuck, the neo-classical House of the painter Franz von Stuck

*Stuck Villa and Art Nouveau Museum (Jugendstilmuseum) N/O20

Location
Prinzregentenstrasse 60

Buses
51, 55

Tram
18

Opening times
Only for special exhibitions

This neo-classical villa was built by the painter Franz von Stuck in 1897–98 and enlarged in 1914 by the addition of an annex containing studios. The interior decoration, designed by Stuck himself, is very characteristic of the turn of the century.
The villa now houses the Art Nouvea (Jugendstil) Museum, with pictures, graphic art, furniture and applied art of the period between 1890 and 1910, including many of Stuck's own works.
Associated with the museum is a large specialised library.

Theatre: Bavarian State

Location
Max-Joseph-Platz

U-Bahn
Marienplatz

S-Bahn
Marienplatz

Adjoining the National Theatre and forming part of the complex of the Residenz, the Bavarian State Theatre, or New Residenz Theatre, is in Max Joseph Platz. It was built between 1948 and 1951 on the site where previously stood the Old Residenz Theatre (see Cuvilliés Theatre) which had been destroyed by fire in 1944. The New Residenz Theatre specialises in Classical productions.

Theatre Museum (Theatermuseum) N18

Location
Galeriestrasse 4 (entrance from Hofgarten arcades)

U-Bahn
Odeonsplatz

Opening times
Only for special exhibitions: Tue.–Thu. 9 a.m.–midday and 1–4.30 p.m., Fri. 9 a.m.–midday and 1–3.30 p.m.

The Theatre Museum has a collection of material on the history of the theatre world-wide which is unique in Germany. It includes sketches of stage sets, figurines, medals, manuscripts and portraits of actors and actresses, and has associated with it a specialised library of 40,000 volumes. The museum puts on periodic special exhibitions on particular subjects, calling on its own resources and on loan material.
The museum also runs a special service (Münchner Spielplan, or Munich Repertoire) of information on current performances at all Munich theatres (photographs, programmes, texts, librettos).
The Museum was founded by Clara Ziegler (1844–1909), an actress in the Court company. It is housed in the old Electoral Gallery (by Lespilliez, 1780–81).

**Theatinerkirche (Theatine Church of St Cajetan) N19

Location
Theatinerstrasse 22

U-Bahn
Odeonsplatz

The Theatinerkirche, dedicated to St Cajetan, founder of the Theatine Order, stands just to the west of the Feldherrnhalle. A basilica in the style of Italian High Baroque, it is one of Munich's finest churches, and together wth the Frauenkirche (see entry) and St Peter's Church (see entry) is one of the city's most prominent landmarks.
The church was founded by Elector Ferdinand Maria and his wife Henrietta Adelaide in thanksgiving for the birth of the son

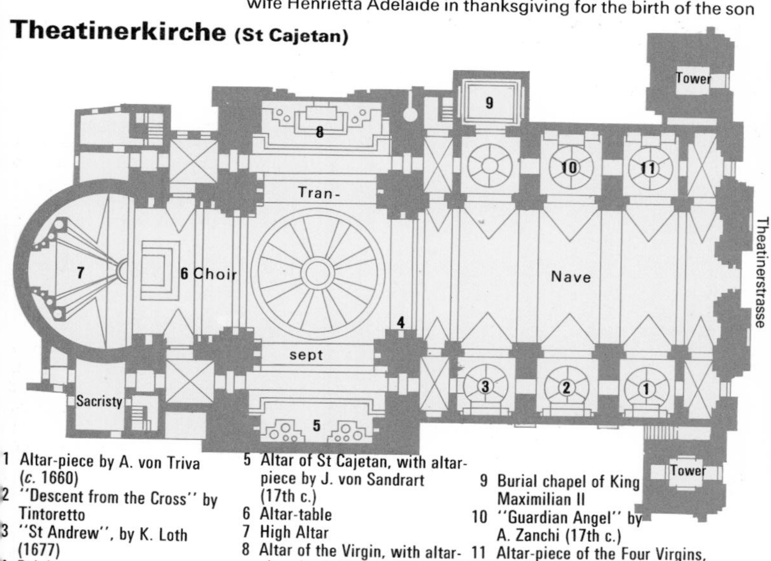

Theatinerkirche (St Cajetan)

1 Altar-piece by A. von Triva (*c.* 1660)
2 "Descent from the Cross" by Tintoretto
3 "St Andrew", by K. Loth (1677)
4 Pulpit
5 Altar of St Cajetan, with altar-piece by J. von Sandrart (17th c.)
6 Altar-table
7 High Altar
8 Altar of the Virgin, with altar-piece by C. Cignani (1676)
9 Burial chapel of King Maximilian II
10 "Guardian Angel" by A. Zanchi (17th c.)
11 Altar-piece of the Four Virgins, by P. Liberi (17th c.)

Opening times
Ducal Vault: Spring to 2 Nov., Mon.–Fri. 10 a.m.–1 p.m. and 3–5 p.m., Sat. 10 a.m.–3 p.m.

and heir they had long desired, Max Emanuel. After its consecration the church, which also served as a Court church, was assigned to the Theatine Order. Since 1954 it has been served by Benedictines.
The church (Latin cross plan, domed) was designed by the Italian architect Agostino Barelli, who also directed the first stage of its building (1663–69). His successor Enrico Zuccalli completed the 71 m (233 ft) high dome, decorated the interior and built the twin towers which had not been provided for in Barelli's plan; this second building phase was completed by 1690. The façade was completed only in the reign of Maximilian III Joseph, in 1765–68; in the style of the Late Rococo period, it was designed by François Cuvilliés and his son.

Façade

The façade with its twin towers is clearly articulated both vertically and horizontally. The marble statues in the niches (SS. Ferdinand, Adelheid, Maximilian and Cajetan) are by Roman Boos. The towers have serpentine ornament just below their domed tops. The massive central dome is topped by a lantern with a lion weather-vane.

Interior

The interior is dominated by the tall round-headed arches of the barrel vaulting and the dome over the crossing. The whole interior surface is washed in white, with rich stucco ornament by Giovanni Antonio Viscardi.
Notable features of the interior:
The High Altar, with a picture, "The Virgin enthroned, with Angels" (1646), by Caspar de Crayer, a pupil of Rubens.
The Altar of the Virgin (right transept), with a "Holy Kinship" by Cignani (1676) and an "Annunciation" by Desmarées (on altar-table).
The Altar of St Cajetan (left transept), with a painting by Sandrart, "Intercession of St Cajetan during the Plague in Naples".
The magnificent black pulpit by Andreas Faistenberger (1685–90).
In the Ducal Burial Vault under the High Altar are the tombs of members of the House of Wittelsbach, including Ferdinand Maria, Max Emanuel, Charles Albert, Maximilian III Joseph and Charles Theodore, Kings Maximilian I and Otto of Greece, Prince Regent Luitpold and Crown Prince Rupert.

*Trinity Church (Dreifaltigkeitskirche) N18

Location
Pacellistrasse 6

S-Bahn
Karlsplatz

During the War of the Spanish Succession a young woman of Munich, Anna Maria Lindtmayr, prophesied that a divine judgment would fall on the city, which would be saved only if a vow were made to build a church. Accordingly when Munich was threatened with fire and plunder in 1704 representatives of the nobility, clergy and citizenry made a solemn vow in the Frauenkirche "to cause to be built in our city a church with several altars for the greater worship of the Most Holy Trinity". The church was designed by the Court Architect, Giovanni Antonio Viscardi, and the foundation-stone was laid in 1711. After Viscardi's death in 1713 the church was completed by Ettenhofer and Zuccalli, with a tower which had not been included in the original plan.

The Theatinerkirche (right) and Feldherrnhalle (left)

"Raree-show" in the Valentin Museum

Façade

The façade was the first convex church façade in Bavaria. It is notable for its plastic sense of movement, vigorous rhythm and clear articulation.
In a niche on the pediment is a figure of St Michael by Josef Fichtl (1726).

Interior

The interior is cruciform, with a square central area and a longer north arm containing the choir.
The High Altar (1721–28) is by Fichtl; the altar-piece (by Johann Andreas Wolff and Johannes Degler, 1716–17), depicting the Trinity over the City of Munich, was presented to the church by the Elector.
On the right-hand side altar are a painting of St Joseph by Joseph Ruffini (1718) and figures of St John and St Peter by Andreas Faistenberger.
On the left-hand side altar can be seen a painting of St Teresa by Degler and figures of St John of the Cross and Elijah by Balthasar Ableithner.
The impressive frescoes are by Cosmas Damian Asam (1715): in the dome the Trinity (with a self-portrait of the artist – on right, by the north-east window), in the transept the Baptism of Christ and the Transfiguration.

Valentin Museum (Valentin-Musäum) O18

Location
Isartor

S-Bahn
Isartor

Opening times
Mon., Tue. and Sat.
11.1 a.m.–5.29 p.m.,
Sun. 10.1 a.m.–5.29 p.m.

Closed
Wed.–Fri.

The Valentin Museum – which makes a point of the unusual spelling Musäum – commemorates the popular actor Karl Valentin (1882–1948), a Munich "character" noted for his witty and humorous dialogues. In addition to a "raree-show" of pictures, curios and humorous documents there is a folk-singers' café with turn-of-the-century décor.
In keeping with the quirky character of the museum the opening times are equally off-beat. It opens its doors on Mondays, Tuesdays and Saturdays at one minute after eleven precisely (on Sundays at one minute after ten) and closes at one minute before half-past five precisely.

Viktualienmarkt (Food Market) O18

U-Bahn
Marienplatz

S-Bahn
Marienplatz

The market which has been held in this square since 1807 is a very characteristic feature of Munich life. In addition to numbers of stalls selling fruit and vegetables, flowers, dairy produce, eggs and poultry there are market halls for meat, fish and game. The market is a scene of activity throughout the day. The market women dance on Shrove Tuesday every year during the carnival celebrations.
There are a number of fountains with statues of celebrated Munich figures who are still remembered with affection – the popular actor Karl Valentin (1882–1948), the actress Liesl Karlstadt (1892–1960), who played opposite him for many years, the folk-singer Weiss Ferdl (1883–1949), Elise Aulinger (1891–1965), Roider Jakl (1906–75) and Ida Schumacher (1895–1956).

The Viktualienmarkt (in the background St Peter's Church and the Frauenkirche) ▶

HOLLAND

The Wittelsbach Fountion in Lenbachplatz

*West Park P/Q13–15

Location
Untersendling district

U-Bahn
Westpark

S-Bahn
Heimeranplatz

Buses
31, 32, 33

The West Park, laid out for the 4th International Garden Show (IGA 83), lies some 3 km (2 miles) south-west of the Central Station. Beautifully designed and planted, it has an area of some 720,000 sq. m (178 acres) and extends for about 2 km (1¼ miles) from east to west, divided into an eastern and a western half by Garmischer Strasse. A narrow-gauge railway runs through the park, with its flower-beds, lawns and lakes, playgrounds, a Kneipp treatment establishment, a lakeside theatre and a restaurant and café.

Wittelsbacher-Platz N18

U-Bahn
Odeonsplatz

Rectangular in plan and uniform in style, the Wittelsbacher-Platz has something of the effect of a great hall. It is surrounded by elegant and palatial buildings designed by Leo von Klenze – the Palais Arco-Zinneberg (1820) on the west side and the Wittelsbacher-Palais (1825) on the north side, which was Klenze's home for 25 years and was later acquired by Prince Ludwig Ferdinand of Wittelsbach; it is now the head office of the Siemens corporation.
In the centre of the square is an equestrian statue of Elector Maximilian I, a fine neo-classical work by Thorvaldsen (1830).

Wittelsbach Fountain (Wittelsbacher-Brunnen)

N17

Munich's most celebrated fountain, a neo-classical work by the sculptor Adolf von Hildebrandt (1893–95), is picturesquely situated on the east side of Lenbachplatz, in front of the clumps of trees in Maximiliansplatz. In its large circular basin, with a high fountain base supporting two smaller basins, are two pieces of sculpture – a youth on a water-horse hurling a boulder and a women riding on another aquatic animal and pouring out water from a vessel (symbolising the power and beneficence of water). The fountain was erected to commemorate the completion of the new municipal water-supply system, a major contribution to the cost being made by the Wittelsbachs in gratitude for the supply of water to the Residence.

Location
Lenbachplatz

U-Bahn
Hauptbahnhof

S-Bahn
Karlsplatz

**Zoo

See Hellabrunn Zoo

Practical Information

Airlines

All the major airlines have offices in Munich. The following is a selection.

Aer Lingus,
Oskar-von-Miller-Ring 36, tel. 28 83 20

Air France,
Theatinerstrasse 23, Odeonsplatz, tel. 2 10 67

British Airways,
Promenadeplatz 10, tel. 29 11 21

Hapag-Lloyd,
Riem Airport, tel. 9 25 31

Iberia,
Schwanthalerstrasse 16, tel. 59 75 81

KLM,
Sendlinger Strasse 37, tel. 26 80 26

Lufthansa,
Lenbachplatz 1, tel. 5 11 30

PanAm,
Lenbachplatz 3, tel. 55 81 71

Sabena,
Petersplatz 10, tel. 2 60 50 54

SAS,
Pacellistrasse 8/III, tel. 22 06 36

Swissair,
Marienplatz 21, tel. 23 63 0

TWA,
F & G Reise GmbH, Ottostrasse 1, tel. 59 76 43

Airport

Munich's airport, München-Riem, is 8 km (5 miles) east of the city centre. It has direct connections with many European cities and links with the international network of air services.
When the large new airport north of the city comes into operation Riem Airport will be closed.

Information

For flight information tel. 92 11-21 27.

Tourist Office

There is a branch of the City Tourist Office (Fremdenverkehrsamt) in the Arrival Hall: tel. 90 72 56 and 23 91-2 66.
Open Mon.–Sat. 8.30 a.m.–10 p.m., Sun. 1–9 p.m.

The Tourist Office does not provide flight information and cannot handle telephone requests for hotel bookings.

Luggage trolleys

Luggage trolleys can be hired for a fee.

Airport bus

Departures from Central Station (north side, Arnulfstrasse) every 20 minutes from 5.40 a.m. to 8.40 p.m.

Antiques

Munich has more than 300 antique-dealers, handling articles of many different styles and periods, including many unusual and out-of-the-way items. They range from the most elegant and exclusive establishments to a variety of low-price junk-shops. A list of dealers, with their addresses and telephone numbers (but usually without any indication of their particular line), can be found in the "yellow pages" telephone book.
Antique shops in Schwabing: Amalienstrasse, Türkenstrasse, Barer Strasse, Kurfürstenstrasse, Hohenzollernstrasse. In the city centre: Ottostrasse, Lenbachplatz, Promenadenstrasse, Promenadeplatz, Theatinerstrasse, Residenzstrasse, Westenrieder Strasse.

Antique fairs and markets

German Art and Antiques Fair, held annually in late autumn in the Haus der Kunst.
Art and antiques fairs run by dealers three times a year in the German Museum.
Antique markets, offering a great variety of wares, held from time to time in beer-cellars.
Auer Dult (see A to Z): fairs for the sale of antiques, folk art and junk.

Banks

Opening times

Most banks and savings banks are open from 8.30 a.m. to 4 p.m., on Thursday to 5.30 p.m. Some close at lunchtime.

Changing money

Money can be changed at all banks and savings banks during normal opening hours.

Late opening

The exchange offices of the Deutsche Verkehrs-Kredit-Bank are open after normal banking hours.
Office in Central Station open 6 a.m.–11.30 p.m.
Office at airport open 7 a.m.–8.30 p.m.

Special rates

Special rates are given for all Eastern European and exotic currencies by the Wechselstube (Exchange Office) L. Schwarcz, Schillerstrasse 3A (at Central Station), tel. 59 82 36. Open Mon.–Fri. 8 a.m.–6 p.m.

Bavaria Film Tour

From 1 April to 31 October visitors can see round the Bavaria Film City in Geiselgasteig (Bavaria Atelier GmbH, Bavariafilm-

platz 7, Geiselgasteig). The "Film Express" tours the studios daily from 9 a.m. to 4 p.m.
For groups of 20 or more it is advisable to make an appointment: tel. (089) 64 99-3 04.
Tram 25; U-Bahn U 8.

Beer-gardens and beer-cellars

Munich's beer-gardens – large open-air establishments where the customers sit at tables set in the shade of chestnut trees and drink their beer in litre tankards (*masskrüge*) – are open in the evening and at week-ends during the warmer months. The beer may be accompanied by a snack (which you can take in with you) of pretzels, bread, horse-radish, sausage, meat loaf (*leberkäs*) or cheese.
Since the older beer-gardens are near the cellars in which the breweries keep their beer they are known as beer-cellars or simply as cellars – though the customers do not actually sit in the cellar. Many beer-gardens also have rooms where drinkers can sit during the winter. Every year during Lent (4th and 3rd weeks before Easter) strong dark beers (18–19 per cent wort content) are served, with names ending in *-ator*. In spite of their high alcohol content they are light and attractive to drink: caution, therefore, is advisable, lest you drink too much without being aware of it.
The following are some of the best-known Munich beer-gardens:

Augustinerkeller,
Arnulfstrasse 52 (near Central Station)
U- and S-Bahn: Hauptbahnhof

Aumeister,
Sondermeierstrasse 1 (north side of Englischer Garten; approach from Mittlerer Ring)
Bus: 44

Chinesischer Turm,
Englischer Garten
U-Bahn: Giselastrasse

Hackerkeller,
Theresienhöhe 4
S-Bahn: Hackerbrücke

Hirschau,
Gysslingstrasse 7, Englischer Garten (approach from Mittlerer Ring)
Bus: 44

Hirschgarten,
Hirschgartenstrasse 1
S-Bahn: Laim

Hofbräukeller,
Innere Wiener Strasse 19 (near Maximilianeum)
Trams: 14, 18, 19
Buses: 51, 53, 55

In a Munich beer-garden

Löwenbräukeller,
Nymphenburger Strasse 2 (on Stiglmaierplatz)
U-Bahn: Königsplatz

Metzgerwirt,
Nördliche Auffahrtsallee 69 (Nymphenburg)
Tram: 12
Bus: 41

Osterwaldgarten,
Keferstrasse 12 (Schwabing)
U-Bahn: Münchener Freiheit

Pschorrkeller,
Theresienhöhe 7
S-Bahn: Hackerbrücke

Salvatorkeller,
Hochstrasse 77 (on Nockherberg)
Trams: 15, 25, 27
Bus: 51

Seehaus-Biergarten,
Englischer Garten (on lake)
Bus: 44

Boutiques

Fashionable and nostalgic clothes, modern furniture, arts and crafts, "way-out" gifts – all these are to be found in

Schwabing's numerous boutiques (in the University quarter, Hohenzollernstrasse, Leopoldstrasse, Haimhauser Strasse), as well as in shops in the city centre.
A number of internationally famed fashion houses have shops in the more elegant and fashionable streets in the city centre (Maximilianstrasse, Promenadeplatz, Wurzerstrasse).

Cabarets

See Night Life.

Camping

Information

Information about camping can be obtained from the Deutscher Camping club, Mandlstrasse 28, tel. 33 40 21.

Langwieder See camping site

Eschenrieder Strasse 119 (8 km (5 miles) from Munich on Stuttgart motorway), tel. 8 14 15 66
Open 1 April to 15 October

Obermenzing camping site

Lochhausener Strasse 59, tel. 8 11 22 35
Buses: 75, 76
Open all year

Thalkirchen camping site

Zentralländstrasse 49 (near Hellabrunn Zoo), tel. 7 23 17 07
Buses: 31, 57, 66
Open mid March to end of October

Camping Guide

Detailed information about camping sites in and around Munich is given in the ADAC-Campingführer (Camping Guide), a new edition of which appears annually.

Car hire

Car hire firms are listed in the "yellow pages" telephone book under the heading "Autovermietung".

Chemists

Medicines can be obtained at all times, thanks to the emergency service organised by Munich pharmacies, under which certain shops remain open at night and on Sundays and public holidays. The addresses and telephone numbers of such pharmacies in the various districts are given in the Friday edition of the "Münchner Stadtanzeiger" (a supplement to the "Süddeutsche Zeitung") for the coming week; alternatively they can be obtained by telephoning 59 44 75. When a chemist's shop is closed it displays a notice giving the address of the nearest duty pharmacy.

Church services

The times of services in the churches of various denominations are given every Friday in the newspapers.

Roman Catholic churches

Frauenkirche (Cathedral),
Frauenplatz 1
Sundays and public holidays at 6.30, 8, 9.30, 11 a.m., midday and 6 p.m.; Saturdays at 5.30 p.m.

St Peter's Church (Peterskirche),
Rindermarkt 1
Sundays and public holidays at 7, 8, 9, 10.15, 11.15 a.m., midday and 6.30 p.m.; Saturdays at 6 p.m.

Church of the Holy Ghost (Heiliggeistkirche),
Tal 77
Sundays and public holidays at 6.30, 7.30, 9, 10, 11 a.m. and 7 p.m.; Saturdays at 5.30 p.m.

Theatinerkirche,
Theatinerstrasse 22
Sundays and public holidays at 8, 9.15, 10.30 a.m., midday and 6.30 p.m.; Saturdays at 5.30 p.m.

St Michael's Church (Michaelskirche),
Neuhauser Strasse 52
Sundays and public holidays at 6, 7, 8, 9, 10.30, 11.30 a.m. and 6 p.m.; Saturdays at 6 p.m.

Protestant churches

St Matthew's Church (Matthäuskirche),
Nussbaumstrasse 1 (Sendlinger-Tor-Platz)
Sundays at 8.30 and 10 a.m.

St Mark's Church (Markuskirche),
Gabelsbergerstrasse 6
Sundays at 9.30 and 11.15 a.m.

Synagogue

Synagogue,
Reichenbachstrasse 27

Circus

Zirkus Krone,
Marsstrasse 43

Munich has its own circus, the internationally renowned Zirkus Krone, which presents a winter season (December to March) of superb artistry and skill in its own premises. During the rest of the year it is on tour in Europe and overseas.
The Zirkus Krone building in Marsstrasse, in the form of a big top, was erected in 1962. When the circus is on tour the building is used for pop concerts, sporting events and political meetings. – In front of the building can be seen a bronze statue of the world-famed clown Charlie Rivel (1896–1983).

Concerts

See Music

Consulates

United Kingdom

Consulate-General,
Amalienstrasse 62, tel. 39 40 15
U-Bahn: Universität

United States

Consulate-General,
Königinstrasse 5, tel. 2 30 11
U-Bahn: Odeonsplatz
Buses: 53, 55

Canada

Consulate-General,
Maximiliansplatz 9, tel. 55 85 31
Bus: 55

Cultural institutions

Amerika-Haus

Karolinenplatz 3, tel. 59 53 67
U-Bahn: Odeonsplatz

British Council

Bruderstrasse 7/III, tel. 22 33 26
Buses: 53, 55

Goethe-Institut

Lenbachplatz 3, tel. 5 99 91
S-Bahn: Karlsplatz

Emergency calls

Police and emergency call throughout Germany: 110.

See also Useful Telephone Numbers on last page of Guide.

Events

January

7 January to Ash Wednesday: Fasching, the Shrovetide carnival.

February

Fasching Sunday: "Munich plays the fool" from 1 to 4 p.m. in the squares in the city centre, which are decorated for the occasion.
A special feature of the Fasching celebrations which occurs only every seven years is the Schäfflertanz, a gay dance danced by members of the Coopers' Guild, wearing colourful costumes and holding garlands of leaves.
The custom, which is first mentioned in 1463, originated in a time of plague, when the coopers performed their dance in order to cheer up the citizens of Munich, afraid to venture into the streets for fear of the plague.

The Schäfflertanz

March

Beginning of March: St Joseph's Day; the strong spring-brewed beer is drunk for the first time.

April

From about 25 April to 3 May: Maidult (Junk Fair) in the Mariahilfplatz in the Au district.
Spring Festival on the Theresienwiese.

May

Corpus Christi (second Thursday after Whitsun): procession through the city.
Drinking of the "Maibock" ("May beer"); ceremonial broaching of the first barrel in the Hofbräuhaus.

June

3rd week in June: Schwabing Week (painting, sculpture, literature, music, drama, experimental art).
Baroque concerts in the Baroque Hall of Schleissheim Palace every Friday, Saturday and Sunday in June–July.

July

25 July to 2 August: Jakobidult (St James's Fair) in the Au district.
Magdalenenfest (Magdalene Fair) in the Hirschgarten.
Nymphenburg Summer Festival (concerts in Nymphenburg Palace).
Open Festival.

August

Opera Festival.
Performances by the Munich Chamber Opera in the Brunnenhof of the Residence.
Dachau Fair.

The Oktoberfest in full swing

September

First Sunday and Monday: Horse Fair in Keferloh (22 km (14 miles) east of Munich).
Freising Fair.

October

Oktoberfest (October Festival; begins at end of September). At 11 a.m. on first day, ceremonial entry of the breweries and Festival "hosts"; at 8 p.m. Folklore International in the Zirkus Krone.
Mid October: Herbst Dult (Autumn Fair) in the Au district.
First Sunday of Oktoberfest: Costume and Marksmen's Parade at 10 a.m.

November

St Leonard's Ride (procession, with blessing of horses) at Bad Tölz and elsewhere.

December

Christkindl- und Kripperlmarkt (Christ Child and Manger Fair) on the Marienplatz and in front of the Frauenkirche, with Christmas music in the evening.

Excursions

For those who want to escape from the rush and bustle of the city Munich offers a wide range of possibilities. The Federal Railways and private bus companies operate trips to many of the most popular destinations in Upper Bavaria, and the city transport authorities have waymarked a hundred or so attractive country walks in the surrounding area, starting from and returning to S-Bahn stations.

Rail excursions

The "Glass Train" run by the Federal Railways goes to many attractive places which are difficult to get to by public transport in the normal way – the Chiemsee and Königssee, Rothenburg ob der Tauber, the Bavarian Forest, the Salzkammergut, Kirchberg in Tirol and many more. There is also a very reasonable "package" covering the journey to Garmisch-Partenkirchen and the ascent of the Zugspitze, Germany's highest mountain; in winter this trip is available for skiers. Information from Federal Railways.

Coach excursions

The Autobus-Fahrten-Gemeinschaft (Sophienstrasse 2, tel. 55 80 61) operates coach trips to King Ludwig II's castles of Linderhof, Neuschwanstein and Herrenchiemsee, to Berchtesgaden, Salzburg and Tirol, on the Romantische Strasse (Romantic Road) top Rothenburg ob der Tauber and Regensburg and to Walhalla, the Bavarian Temple of Fame.
Information also from Reisebüro abr, tel. 59 04–0; Isaria-Reisen, tel. 2 37 23–0; or Elite-Reisen, tel. 42 27 41.

Walks

The Munich transport authorities (MVV) have provided excellent facilities for walkers in the Munich region. The S-Bahn stations display maps suggesting walks in the area, including both short trips and longer excursions, and waymarked routes take in not only tourist sights such as castles and palaces, churches and monasteries, but also pleasant Bavarian wayside inns. Among stations offering the most attractive walks are Herrsching, Tutzing, Starnberg, Mühltal, Gauting, Grafrath, Dachau, Freising, Ebersberg, Aying, Poing (game reserve) and Markt Schwaben.
A map showing rail routes in the Munich region is displayed in all S-Bahn and U-Bahn stations.

Food

Bavarian food does not, in general, enjoy a high reputation in Germany: it is criticised as lacking in imagination and over-given to dumplings and cabbage. In fact it offers a whole range of substantial, tasty and appetising dishes which visitors should on no account fail to sample. In addition to typically Bavarian dishes there are a number from other regions, notably Tirol and Swabia, which have been taken into Bavarian cuisine.
The Bavarians are great meat-eaters, but less fond of vegetables.
Much use is made of thyme, bay leaves and nutmeg for seasoning. Cakes and pastries are a favourite indulgence.

Brotzeit:

Brotzeit (bread time) is a quick snack which, depending on hunger, thirst and appetite, may include:

Leberkäs
(liver cheese: meat loaf)

Crusty brown rolls containing roast beef, pork, bacon, onions, marjoram and nutmeg – but no liver.

Horse-radish

The horse-radish (*radi*) is cut into thin slices and salted to make it "weep".

Weisswürste
(white sausages)

These delicious sausages, invented by a Munich butcher on Fasching Sunday in 1857, contain veal, bacon, lemon and parsley, and are eaten with sweet Bavarian mustard and pretzels. They are never eaten after midday: the sausages, it is held, must never hear the clock strike noon.

Obatzta — Cheese (Camembert or Gervais) mixed with chopped onions, pepper, paprika, caraway seed, yolk of egg, butter and salt.

Soups

Authentically Bavarian soups are:

Leberknödelsuppe (liver dumpling soup) — Meat stock with dumplings made of flour, liver, breadcrumbs, spleen, onions, garlic, marjoram, pepper and salt.

Griessnockerlsuppe (semolina dumpling soup) — Meat stock with elongated semolina dumplings.

Meat dishes:

Tellerfleisch — Beef cooked in meat stock and cut into slices.

Tafelspitz — Stewed loin of beef, usually eaten with horse-radish (originally an Austrian dish).

Tiroler Geröstel — Boiled meat cut into small pieces and fried with potatoes and egg.

Kalbsschäuferl — Slices of shoulder of veal, stewed.

Kalbsvögerl — Stewed veal, rolled and stuffed with bacon and gherkins.

Kalbshaxe, Schweinshaxe (knuckle of veal or pork) — These are among the best and best-known Munich specialties. The meat is skinned, washed, salted and peppered, and then fried or grilled, and eaten with cabbage and dumplings.

Kaiserfleisch — Spare rib of pork, lightly cured, roasted or boiled. Known elsewhere as Kasseler Rippenspeer.

G'selcht's — A general term applied to various kinds of smoked meat.

Fleischpflanzl — Fried meat balls, eaten with potato salad.

Lüngerl — Lights, cut into thin strips, cooked in a sauce and served with bread dumplings.

Beuscherl — Calf's lights, with the heart and spleen.

Krautwickerl — Rolled white cabbage leaves stuffed with meat.

Hendl — Chicken.

Sausages:

In addition to the white sausages already mentioned a number of other kinds are popular in Munich:

Schweinswürstl (pork sausages) — Eaten with sauerkraut and mustard.

G'schwollne — Sausages of finely minced veal, fried in butter. Also known as wollwürste.

Also known as Regensburger: a small spicy sausage of minced beef and pork. — Dicke

Made from calf's sweetbread and spleen, cut into slices, coated with breadcrumbs and fried. — Milzwurst

Otherwise known as Lyoner: made from beef, pork and veal with pistachio nuts. — Leoni

Vegetables, etc.:

Shredded white cabbage, salted and cooked with bacon and juniper berries. — Sauerkraut

Potato fritters. — Reiberdatschi

Bread dumplings made with parsley, onion and egg. Eaten with knuckle of veal or pork, roast pork and mushrooms. — Semmelknödel

Cakes and pastries

If you have a sweet tooth you will do well in Bavaria, which is renowned for its cakes and pastries.

Sweet yeast dumplings cooked in milk, usually accompanied by a vanilla sauce. — Dampfnudeln

Fried yeast dumplings. — Rohrnudeln

Doughnuts. — Schmalznudeln

Round yeast cakes, drawn out thin in the middle. — Aus'zog'ne

Sliced apples baked in pancake dough. — Apfelküchert, Apfelradl

Fritters. — Krapfen

A succulent plum cake made with yeast dough, baked in large cake-tins and sold in slices. — Zwetschgndatschi

Yeast dough rolled out and stretched, then rolled up with various fillings – apples, curd cheese, meat, etc. — Strudel

Galleries

In addition to the large state and municipal galleries and museums Munich has many small private galleries selling pictures and other works of art. The addresses and sometimes an indication of the particular interests of these private galleries can be found in the "yellow pages" telephone book under the headings "Galerien", "Kunsthandlungen", "Antiquitäten", "Antiquariate" and "Bilder".

Hotels

Hotel-Verzeichnis (Hotel List)

A list of Munich's hotels, guest-houses and other accommodation for visitors, giving the number of beds, facilities provided and tariffs, is published annually by the Tourist Office (postal address: Postfach, 8000 München 1, Rindermarkt 5/II; branches in Central Station and at airport; tel. 2 39 11). The list is also published in the Tourist Office's "Official Monthly Programme" ("Offizielles Monatsprogramm"), obtainable from bookshops and newspaper kiosks.

Room booking service

In addition to providing information the Tourist Office will also make hotel bookings on written application (which must be made in plenty of time – in the case of parties of 15 or more at least two weeks in advance).

City centre

Amba (no rest.), Arnulfstrasse 20, 160 beds
Ambassador, Mozartstrasse 4, 100 beds
Ariston (no rest.), Unsöldstrasse 10, 112 beds
*Bayerischer Hof & Palais Montgelas, Promenadeplatz 2–6, 636 beds, swimming-pool, sauna
Bundesbahn-Hotel, in Central Station, Bahnhofplatz 2, 300 beds
Central (no rest.), Schwanthalerstrasse 111, 130 beds
Concorde (no rest.), Herrnstrasse 38, 100 beds
Continental, Max-Joseph-Platz 5, 250 beds
Deutscher Kaiser, Arnulfstrasse 2, 300 beds
Drei Löwen, Schillerstrasse 8, 200 beds
Eden-Hotel Wolff, Arnulfstrasse 4–8, 300 beds
Excelsior, Schützenstrasse 11, 170 beds
Haberstock, Schillerstrasse 4, 114 beds
*Hilton, Am Tucherpark 7, 950 beds, swimming-pool, sauna
*Königshof, Karlsplatz 25, 200 beds
Metropol, Bayerstrasse 43, 368 beds
Reinbold, Adolf-Kolping-Strasse 11, 110 beds
Schlicker, Tal 74, 100 beds
Torbräu, Tal 37, 165 beds
*Vier Jahreszeiten Kempinski, Maximilianstrasse 17, 565 beds, swimming-pool, sauna; *Walterspiel Restaurant

Bogenhausen

Arabella, Arabellastrasse 5, 550 beds, swimming-pool
Crest, Effnerstrasse 99, 300 beds
*Sheraton, Arabellastrasse 6, 1300 beds, swimming-pool, sauna

Haidhausen

Penta, Hochstrasse 3, 1160 beds, swimming-pool

Neuperlach

Orbis, Karl-Marx-Ring 87, 326 beds, swimming-pool (open-air)

Oberwiesenfeld

Olympiapark, Helene-Mayer-Ring 12, 200 beds, swimming-pool

Schwabing

Holiday Inn, Leopoldstrasse 194, 716 beds, roofed swimming-pool; Yellow Submarine night club
Residence, Artur-Kutscher-Platz 4, 300 beds, swimming-pool
Tourotel, Domagkstrasse 26, 300 beds, swimming-pool
Motel Vitalis, Kathi-Kobus-Strasse 24, 250 beds, outdoor swimming-pool

Information

Tourist Office

Fremdenverkehrsamt,
Postfach, 8000 München,
telex 5 24 80 1 frast d,
tel. (089) 23 91-1

Tourist Office in Central Station

At south exit (Bayerstrasse)
Tel. 23 91-2 56 and 2 57
Open Mon.–Sat. 8 a.m.–11 p.m., Sun. 1–9.30 p.m.
Room booking service (not by telephone), information, leaflets

Tourist Office at Airport

Arrival Hall
Tel. 90 72 56 and 23 91-2 66
Open Mon.–Sat. 8.30 a.m.–10 p.m., Sun. 1–9 p.m.
Room booking service (not by telephone); not flight information

Upper Bavarian Tourist Office

Fremdenverkehrsverband München-Oberbayern,
Sonnenstrasse 10/III, tel. 59 73 47
Open Mon.–Fri. 8 a.m.–midday and 1–4 p.m.
Information and advice on excursions in surrounding area

Information for young people

Jugend-Informations-Zentrum (Youth Information Centre),
Paul-Heyse-Strasse 22, tel. 53 16 55
Open Mon.–Fri. 11 a.m.–7 p.m., Sat. 11 a.m.–5 p.m.; closed Sun. and public holidays

City Press and Information Office

Presse- und Informationsstelle der Stadt München,
Rathaus, Marienplatz, Room 241, tel. 2 33/64 47
Open Mon.–Thu. 7.15 a.m.–3.45 p.m., Fri. 7.15 a.m.–2 p.m.

City Information Office

Shopping centre, Karlsplatz (Stachus),
tel. 2 33-82 42 and 55 44 59
Open Mon.–Fri. 8 a.m.–6 p.m.; closed Sat., Sun. and public holidays.

Alpine Information Office

Deutscher Alpenverein,
Praterinsel 5, tel. 29 49 40

Libraries and archives

Library of Deutscher Alpenverein,
Alpenvereinshaus,
Praterinsel 5, tel. 29 30 86
S-Bahn: Isartor
A unique collection of literature on the Alps. Only members of the Alpenverein may borrow books.

Bavarian State Archives (Bayerisches Hauptstaatsarchiv),
Schönfeldstrasse 5
Bavarian State Library
See A to Z, State Library

Library of German Museum,
Museumsinsel (Ludwigsbrücke), tel. 2 17 92 24
S-Bahn: Isartor
Open Mon.–Fri. 9 a.m.–5 p.m.
A specialist library on the exact sciences

Library of German Patent Office,
Zweibrückenstrasse 12, tel. 21 91-1
S-Bahn: Isartor
A reference library of 300,000 volumes

International Youth Library
See A to Z, Blutenburg Castle

Municipal Libraries

Central Library, Infanteriestrasse 7A, tel. 19 42 69
Tram: 12
Open Mon., Wed. and Fri. 10 a.m.–7 p.m., Tue. and Thu. 10 a.m.–3 p.m.
Books, periodicals, music, records, cassettes for instruction, recreation and entertainment.
Branch libraries in all parts of the city; travelling libraries with lending points

Music Library (Municipal Libraries),
Salvatorplatz 1, tel. 22 27 04
U-Bahn: Odeonsplatz
S-Bahn: Marienplatz
Open Mon., Wed. and Fri. 2–7 p.m., Tue. and Thu. 10 a.m.–3 p.m.
Music, books, records, tape-recorder studio

Munich and Manuscript Department
(Municipal Libraries),
Hildebrandhaus, Maria-Theresia-Strasse 23, tel. 4 70 20 24
Tram: 18
Open Mon.–Fri. 8 a.m.–3.30 p.m. (reading room only)
Material on Munich, autograph manuscripts, ex-libris

Philatelic Department
(Municipal Libraries),
Pestalozzistrasse 2, tel. 2 33-1
U-Bahn: Sendlinger-Tor-Platz
Open Mon. 8 a.m.–midday, Tue. midday–7 p.m., Thu. and Fri. 8 a.m.–3.30 p.m.
Books and periodicals on philately

Law Department
(Municipal Libraries),
Rathaus, Marienplatz, Room 365, tel. 2 33-82 57
Open Mon.–Fri. 8 a.m.–3.30 p.m. (reading room only)

Municipal Archives (Stadtarchiv),
Winzererstrasse 68, tel. 18 07 46
U-Bahn: Hohenzollernplatz
Open Mon.–Wed. 8.30 a.m.–4 p.m., Thu. 8.30 a.m.–8 p.m., Fri. 8.30 a.m.–2 p.m.
Records of Munich municipal administration from 1265 to the present day

University Library,
Geschwister-Scholl-Platz 1, tel. 21 80-24 31
U-Bahn: Universität
Open (lending and catalogues) Mon.–Fri. 9 a.m.–midday and 1.30–4.30 p.m., Tue. 1.30–6 p.m.; (reading rooms) during term Mon.–Fri. 9 a.m.–7.30 p.m., in vacation Mon.–Fri. 9 a.m.–6.30 p.m.
1,800,000 volumes in all fields of knowledge

Library of University of Technology,
Arcisstrasse 21 (entrance opposite Alte Pinakothek)
Tram: 18
Open (lending) Mon., Tue., Thu. and Fri. 9 a.m.–12.30 p.m. and 1.30–2.30 p.m., Wed. 9 a.m.–12.30 p.m. and 1.30–7.30 p.m., in vacation 1.30–7 p.m.; (reading rooms) Mon.–Thu. 9 a.m.–7.30 p.m., Fri. 9 a.m.–6.30 p.m., in vacation 9 a.m.–5 p.m.
Books, research reports and periodicals on science and technology. Card indexes of articles in specialist journals

Lost property

Municipal Lost Property Office

Ruppertstrasse 19, tel. 2 33-1
U-Bahn: Poccistrasse
Open Mon.–Fri. 8.30 a.m.–midday, Thu. also 2–5.30 p.m.; closed Sat., Sun. and public holidays
Property found in streets and on public transport

Railway Lost Property Office (Central Station)

Bahnhofsplatz 2 (opposite Platform 26), tel. 1 28 58 59
U-Bahn and S-Bahn: Hauptbahnhof
Open Mon.–Fri. 7.30 a.m.–4 p.m.; closed Sun. and public holidays
Property found on trains and railway premises

Railway Lost Property Office (East Station)

Ostbahnhof, tel. 12 88 44 09
S-Bahn: Ostbahnhof
Open Mon.–Fri. 8 a.m.–5.45 p.m., Sat. 8–11.45 a.m.; closed Sun. and public holidays
Property found on S-Bahn

Postal Lost Property Office

Arnulfstrasse 195, Room 105 (Parcel Post Office), tel. 13 95 52
Open Mon.–Fri. 8–11.30 a.m. and 12.30–3 p.m.; closed Sat., Sun. and public holidays
Property found in post offices (including telephone kiosks)

Markets

Food markets

Munich's most celebrated market is the Viktualienmarkt in the city centre (see A to Z).
Other permanent food markets are the Haidhausen Market (Wiener Platz), the Pasing Food Market (Bäckerstrasse 7) and the market in Elisabethplatz, Schwabing.

Christkindlmarkt (Christ Child Market)

This Christmas market, which begins about three weeks before Christmas, has a tradition of many centuries behind it: it first appears in the records in the 14th c. as St Nicholas's Market.

Flea-markets

Flea-markets are held in the Berliner Strasse in northern Schwabing (U-Bahn: Dietlindenstrasse), on the Theresienwiese (S-Bahn: Hackerbrücke), in Mariahilfplatz and on the Münchener Freiheit. The timing of these markets is irregular: for dates, see the daily press.

Antique markets

See Antiques

Motoring

Information

ADAC (Allgemeiner Deutscher Automobil-Club), Ridlerstrasse 35, tel. 51 95-0

DTC (Deutscher Touring Automobilclub), Amalienburgstrasse 23, tel. 8 11 10 48

Pilot service

Head office:
Valpichlerstrasse 9/0, tel. 57 10 16
Pilot stations:
Freimann (Nürnberg motorway), tel. 32 54 17
Ramersdorf (Salzburg motorway), tel. 67 27 55
Unterdill (Garmisch motorway), tel. 75 63 30
Obermenzing (Stuttgart motorway), tel. 8 11 24 12

Breakdown assistance

ADAC (Allgemeiner Deutscher Automobil-Club), tel. 76 76 76
ACE (Auto Club Europa), tel. 53 65 02

Repair garages

These are listed in the "yellow pages" telephone directory under the heading "Autoreparatur".

Car hire

See that entry

Traffic information by radio

See Radio and television

Museum charges

Most museums, galleries and collections charge for admission, though entry is usually free on Sundays and public holidays. Reductions for children, students, parties and artists vary from establishment to establishment: ask at the ticket office. Persons entitled to reductions must of course produce the appropriate card or other evidence of their entitlement.

Music

Opera and ballet

Munich has two theatres in which opera and ballet performances are given, the Gärtnerplatz Theatre and the National Theatre (see A to Z).
Visiting companies from many countries in the world perform operettas, musicals and singspiels in the Deutsches Theater.

Bavarian State Opera (National Theatre),
Max-Joseph-Platz
U-Bahn: Odeonsplatz
S-Bahn: Marienplatz
Advance booking office: Maximilianstrasse 11, tel. 22 13 16
Open Mon.–Fri. 10 a.m.–12.30 p.m. and 3.30–5.30 p.m., Sat. 10 a.m.–12.30 p.m.
Booking begins 7 days before performance
Ticket office opens an hour before the performance

Staatstheater am Gärtnerplatz
U-Bahn: Fraunhoferstrasse

Buses: 52, 56
Trams: 18, 20
Advance booking office: Gärtnerplatz 3, tel. 2 60 32 32
Open Mon.–Fri. 10 a.m.–2.30 p.m. and 3.30–5.30 p.m., Sat. 10 a.m.–12.30 p.m.
Booking begins Sat. for following Wed.–Tue.
Ticket office opens an hour before the performance

Concerts

Munich is one of the leading musical cities in Europe: in addition to the orchestras of the Bavarian State Opera and the Gärtnerplatz Theatre it has the Munich Philharmonic, the Bavarian Radio Symphony Orchestra, the Munich Chamber Orchestra, the Graunke Symphony Orchestra and numerous smaller orchestras, usually specialising in the music of a particular period. There are also regular visits by soloists and ensembles of international reputation, not only in serious music but also in pop and light music.

Herkulessaal, Residence
(entrance in Hofgartenstrasse)
U-Bahn: Odeonsplatz
Orchestral and chamber concerts and solo recitals of classical music; 1500 seats

Congress Hall, German Museum,
Isarinsel
S-Bahn: Isartor
Trams: 18, 20
Concerts and recitals of all kinds; 2400 seats

Villa Stuck,
Prinzregentenstrasse 60
Tram: 18
Buses: 51, 55
Piano, violin and song recitals

Concert Hall of Academy of Music,
Arcisstrasse 12
U-Bahn: Königsplatz
Tram: 18
Recitals by visiting artistes; master classes

Zirkus Krone,
Marsstrasse 43
S-Bahn: Hackerbrücke
Pop concerts

Olympic Hall,
Olympic Park
U-Bahn: Olympiazentrum
Pop concerts

Summer concerts

Summer concerts of classical music with well-known soloists are given in Schleissheim and Nymphenburg Palaces and Blutenburg Castle. For information about these concerts see the daily press or the 'Official Monthly Programme'' published by the Tourist Office (see What's on in Munich).

Serenade concerts

Serenade concerts are given in summer in the Brunnenhof of the Residence. For information see the daily press or the Tourist Office's "Official Monthly Programme".

Church concerts and organ recitals

Concerts and recitals are given throughout the year in the larger churches in Munich. Information: see the daily press or the "Official Monthly Programme".

Newspapers

The Munich daily of national standing is the "Süddeutsche Zeitung" (first published 1945), which replaced the "Münchner Neueste Nachrichten", founded in 1848.
The "Münchner Merkur", which is strong on regional news, succeeded the "Münchner Zeitung" in 1948.
The popular press is represented by the "Münchner Abendzeitung", "tz" and "Bild-Zeitung" (Munich edition).
The fortnightly "Blatt" contains news of fringe groups, political activities and events concerning the "alternative society".

Night life

Discothèques

Drugstore,
Feilitzschstrasse 12, tel. 34 75 31
U-Bahn: Münchener Freiheit

East Side,
Rosenheimer Strasse 32, tel. 48 48 58
S-Bahn: Rosenheimer Platz

P 1,
Prinzregentenstrasse 1 (in Haus der Kunst), tel. 29 42 52

Capt'n Cook,
Occamstrasse 8, tel. 34 49 74

Rumpelkammer,
Trautenwolfstrasse 1, tel. 34 47 93

Why Not,
Brienner Strasse 12, tel. 28 19 68
U-Bahn: Odeonsplatz

Jazz spots

Allotria,
Türkenstrasse 33, tel. 28 58 58
Old-time jazz

Alte Burg,
Bismarckstrasse 21, tel. 33 14 52
Dixie, old-time jazz, skiffle, folk

domicile,
Leopoldstrasse 19, tel. 39 94 51
U-Bahn: Giselastrasse
Modern jazz; guest performances by well known soloists and bands

Schwabinger Spritz'n,
Occamstrasse 15, tel. 39 43 75
Piano "life music"

Night clubs

ba-ba-lu,
Ainmillerstrasse 1, tel. 39 84 64
An elegant night club with international floor shows

Night club in Bayerischer Hof Hotel,
Promenadeplatz 2–6
Sophisticated clientele

Bavaria night club in Hilton Hotel,
Am Tuchermarkt 7, tel. 34 00 51

Cabarets

Münchner Lach- und Schiessgesellschaft,
Haimhauserstrasse/Ursulastrasse, tel. 39 19 97
U-Bahn: Münchener Freiheit
Advance booking from 2 p.m.

Das Münchner Rationaltheater,
Hesseloherstrasse 18, tel. 33 50 40 and 33 40 50
U-Bahn: Münchener Freiheit
Advance booking from 2 p.m. and through ticket agencies
Ticket office open 8 p.m.
Political cabaret

Opening times

Department stores

The department stores in the city centre and their branches in other parts of the city are open Mon.–Fri. 9 a.m.–6.30 p.m., Sat. 8.30 a.m.–2 p.m.; on first Sat. in month 8.30 a.m.–6 p.m.

Other shops

Food and other shops fix their individual opening times. They open between 7 and 9 a.m., often close at lunch-time (though not in the city centre) and close for the day at 6 or 6.30 p.m. Some bakers and butchers are closed on Monday afternoon. On "long Saturday" (the first Saturday in the month) it is left to individual shops to decide whether to stay open in the afternoon; outside the city centre they usually close.

Public holidays

Shops are closed on public holidays (see Public holidays); on Shrove Tuesday they close about midday.

Late shopping

In the Central Station (lower ground floor) there are shops selling food, (including bread, cakes and pastries) books, drugs and toiletries and flowers, some of which open for business as early as 6 a.m. and close as late as 11 p.m.

Post offices

See Postal services

Museums

The state and municipal museums, galleries and collections have different opening times. They are usually closed on Mondays (exceptions: German Museum, Dachau Memorial Site, Hunting Museum, etc.). The museums are closed on some public holidays, particularly on the first days of the great Church festivals.

Banks

See Banks

Opera

See Music

Parking (garages, multi-storey car parks, etc.)

Am Färbergraben
Open Mon.–Sat. 7 a.m.–midnight; closed Sun. and pub. hol.
520 places. Access from Altheimer Eck and Marienplatz

Am Stachus
(Karlsplatz)
Open Mon.–Sat. 7 a.m.–midnight; Sun. and pub. hol. 1 p.m.–midnight
450 places. Access via Goethestrasse, Bayerstrasse/ Schillerstrasse

Fina Parkhaus am Hauptbahnhof
Marsstrasse
Access via Marsstrasse/Lämmerstrasse/Hirtenstrasse

Fina Parkhaus am Hofbräuhaus
Access via Tal, Maximilianstrasse and Altstadtring

Multi-storey car park in Central Station
Open daily 5.30 a.m.–midnight
Entrances in Bayerstrasse and Arnulfstrasse

Tiefgarage vor der Oper
Max-Joseph-Platz
Open Mon.–Sat. 7 a.m.–1 a.m., Sun. and pub. hol. 1 p.m.–1 a.m.
440 places

Am Deutschen Theater
Schwanthalerstrasse 10
Open Mon.–Fri. 6.30 a.m.–10 p.m., Sat. 6.30 a.m.–6 p.m.; closed Sun. and pub. hol.

In der Amalienpassage
Türkenstrasse 84
Open Mon.–Fri. 9 a.m.–1.30 a.m., Sat. 9 a.m.–5 p.m.; closed Sun. and pub. hol.

Multi-storey car park at Riem Airport
Open 24 hours a day.
1466 places; long-term parking facilities

Postal services

Important post offices

Postamt 32,
Bahnhofplatz 1, tel. 55 98-4 06
Always open
Post office savings bank, cheque-cashing and money changing facilities available at night. Letters addressed

"hauptpostlagernd" or "poste restante" are sent here for collection.

Postamt 31,
Bahnhofplatz 2 (in Central Station), tel. 55 98-4 00
Open Mon.–Fri. 7 a.m.–9 p.m., Sat. 8 a.m.–9 p.m.; closed Sun. and pub. hol.

Postamt 1,
Residenzstrasse 2 (near Marienplatz), tel. 21 77-3 02
Open Mon.–Fri. 8 a.m.–6 p.m., early desk 7–8 a.m., late desk 6–6.30 p.m.; Sat. 8 a.m.–midday, early desk 7–8 a.m., late desk midday–1 p.m.

Postamt 87,
Riem Airport, Departure Hall, tel. 90 80 13
Open Mon.–Fri. 8 a.m.–9 p.m., Sat. 8 a.m.–8 p.m., Sun. 10 a.m.–1 p.m. and 2–7.30 p.m.

Postamt 702,
Alfred-Schmid-Strasse 34 (close to Thalkirchen camping site), tel. 76 73-2 35
Open from 8.30 a.m.

Postamt 65,
Bauseweinallee 2 (near Obermenzing camping site), tel. 8 11 29 91
Open Mon.–Fri. 8 a.m.–midday and 3–6 p.m., Sat. 8 a.m.–midday.

Opening times

Post offices within the city are open Mon.–Fri. 8 a.m.–midday and 3–6 p.m., Sat. 8 a.m.–midday.

Public holidays

Bavaria has more public holidays than the rest of the Federal Republic:
New Year's Day (1 January); Epiphany (6 January); Good Friday, Easter Day and Easter Monday; 1 May; Ascension; Whit Sunday and Whit Monday; Corpus Christi; German Unity Day (17 June); Assumption; All Saints (1 November); Day of Prayer and Repentance; first and second day of Christmas.

Public transport

MVV

Munich's U-Bahn (Underground), S-Bahn (Suburban railway system), trams and buses form part of the city's Combined Transport Services (Münchner Verkehrs- und Tarifverbund, MVV). The same tickets (bought from blue ticket machines in U-Bahn and S-Bahn stations, at tram stops, in trams and in many stationers and tobacconists' shops) are used in all these forms of transport.

Tarrif system

The MVV tariff system, complicated in itself, depends on self-service and may thus pose problems for the visitor. If you expect to make several journeys of some length in the course of the

day, the best plan is to buy a 24-hour ticket, which is easy to use. Calculating the fare according to the zonal tariff is more difficult. For journeys of some length the ordinary single tickets are considerably dearer than multiple strip-tickets.
It is important to remember that a ticket is only valid after it has been cancelled in a cancelling machine.

Zonal tariff

Munich city and region are divided into six concentric zones (plans of which are displayed at all stations and stops), and the fare depends on the number of zones traversed in the course of a journey. For different numbers of zones there are ordinary single tickets and strip-tickets, with one section per zone. Within the four outer zones (outside the city) strip-tickets are valid only for a single journey; within the two inner zones the two sections cover more than one journey.
There are ticket cancelling machines at the entrance to U-Bahn and S-Bahn stations and in trams and buses.
Journeys can be broken at any point, but there are time limits on the validity of tickets – 2 hours from time of cancellation for up to 3 zones, 3 hours for up to 7 zones, 4 hours for more than 7 zones.

24-hour tickets

There are 24-hour tickets covering either the whole city area or the whole of the MVV area. They can be bought from the Tourist Office, ticket machines (city area only) and some 250 private sales points throughout the city and region. 24-hour tickets must be signed by the holder, who must be able to produce an identity document, and must be cancelled in a cancelling machine. After cancellation they are valid for any number of journeys within the area.

Short-journey tickets

For short journeys, within limits marked on the zonal plans by white dots, there are special short-journey tickets which cover travel to the next-but-one zonal boundary. They are valid for one hour from time of cancellation; breaks of journey are permitted.

Children's fares

Children under 4 accompanying an adult travel free; for children over 4 and under 15 there is a children's tariff, with fares varying according to the number of zones.

Penalty for non-cancellation of tickets

Passengers found travelling with a ticket which has not been validated by cancellation (or without any ticket) are liable to an on-the-spot fine of 40 DM. Ticket inspectors (who wear plain clothes) show no particular indulgence for visitors.

Two-cities ticket

A two-cities ticket, valid for 24 hours, allows the holder to use tram, bus and rail services in any two of the following German cities: Berlin, Bonn, Bremen, Cologne, Frankfurt am Main, Hamburg, Hannover, Mannheim/Ludwigshafen, Munich, Nürnberg/Fürth, Rhine/Ruhr and Stuttgart. Tickets obtainable at major stations and travel agencies.

Information (MVV)

Münchner Verkehrs- und Tarifverbund,
Thierschstrasse 2, tel. 2 38 03-0

Information (S-Bahn)

Central Station (Platform 26), tel. 55 75 75

Radio and television

The Munich area is served by Bavarian Radio (Bayerischer Rundfunk), which runs both radio and television services. Its headquarters and studios are at Rundfunkplatz 1.

Radio

There are four radio channels, Bayern 1, 2, 3 and 4. Information for tourists is transmitted mainly on Bayern 3.

Bayern 1

Bayern 1 is popular in tone, transmitting programmes of music, entertainment and news.
News: on weekdays half-hourly from 5.30 to 8 a.m., hourly from 9 to 12, at 12.30 and hourly from 1 p.m. to midnight.
Weather reports: at 7 a.m. and 1 and 3 p.m.
Bavarian news: 9.30 a.m. and 5 p.m.
Sport: 11 p.m.
Review of the day: 11 p.m. and midnight.

Bayern 2

Caters for particular interests, with many good musical and cultural programmes. Relays from Munich and Bayreuth Festivals in summer.
News: 6, 7, 8 and 10 a.m., midday, 4, 6, 8 and 10 p.m. and midnight.

Bayern 3
(traffic information)

Popular in tone, with news bulletins every hour on the hour and frequent bulletins of traffic information.
Service information (incorporated in news bulletins):
Conditions on Alpine roads (in winter) and weather for climbers (summer): 7 a.m.
Avalanche report (in winter), weather for travellers (weekdays in summer): 9 a.m.
Weather report (weekdays): 3 p.m.
Weather forecast for road travellers (winter): Mon.–Fri. 3 p.m., Sat. and Sun. 4 p.m.
Weather for holiday-makers (particularly in Bavaria, Austria, northern Italy and Switzerland): 10 p.m.

Bayern 4

The first "classical channel" in the Federal Republic, inaugurated in 1980, with an almost continuous programme of serious music.

Television

Bavarian Television is part of the national network of the Federal Republic, and Bavarian regional programmes are transmitted almost every day in the late afternoon on the national Channel 1. Bavarian Television also runs the Third Programme in Bavaria, mainly devoted to transmissions for schools and regional information.

Raft trips

For many centuries Munich was supplied with timber from the Alpine and pre-Alpine forests by rafts floating it down the Isar. Nowadays rafts are used only for pleasure trips at summer week-ends, from Wolfratshausen to Thalkirchen, going over a number of rapids on the way.

A raft trip down the Isar from Wolfratshausen to Munich

Information

Official Bavarian Travel Bureau (Amtliches Bayerisches Reisebüro), tel. 59 04-0

Rail travel

Travel information

Official Bavarian Travel Bureau
(Amtliches Bayerisches Reisebüro),
Central Station (main concourse),
tel. 59 04-0

City Tourist Office, Central Station
(south entrance), tel. 23 91-2 56

Train information
(including railway buses)

Tel. 59 29 91

S-Bahn information

Tel. 55 75 75

Special trains and excursions

Tel. 1 28/58 46

Information on fares

Tel. 55 41 41

Timetable information

Services to Hannover, Hamburg, Bremen, Berlin and Scandinavia: tel. 1 15 31
Services to Austria and southern Europe: tel. 1 15 32
Services to Tirol, Italy and Switzerland: tel. 1 15 33
Services to Bonn, Cologne, Dortmund, Paris, Holland and

Belgium: tel. 1 15 34
Services to Frankfurt am Main: tel. 1 15 35

Express goods (despatch) and left luggage office

Tel. 1 28-1

Express goods (collection)

Tel. 1 28/66 61

House-to-house luggage service

Tel. 59 34 61

Motorail

Tel. 1 28-8 44 05

Seat reservation

Tel. 1 28-59 94

Railway stations

Central Station (Hauptbahnhof)

A focal point for rail travel within Germany and to other European countries and a junction on the regional S-Bahn and U-Bahn system. Part of the Intercity system, with trains leaving at hourly intervals for many German cities.
Services available: left luggage office and luggage lockers, post office and restaurants in main concourse; Railway Mission and Railway Hotel on south side; Bavarian Travel Bureau, Deutsche Verkehrs-Kredit-Bank exchange office, luggage despatch office, foodshops, bookshop (German and foreign newspapers and periodicals), news cinema.

Starnberg Station (Starnberger Bahnhof)

North wing of Central Station. Trains to Weilheim (Upper Bavaria), Garmisch-Partenkirchen and Mittenwald; restaurant; railway bus station; MVV season ticket office.

Holzkirchen Station (Holzkirchner Bahnhof)

South wing of Central Station. Trains to Wolfratshausen, Bad Tölz, Tegernsee, Schliersee and Bayrischzell.

East Station (Ostbahnhof)

Connected with the Central Station by the S-Bahn tunnel and a line round the city centre.
S-Bahn services to Munich's eastern suburbs; trains to Rosenheim and Salzburg, Kufstein and Mühldorf-Simbach; restaurant, information bureau, bookshop and other shops.

München-Pasing Station

On the west side of the city. S-Bahn station; trains to Weilheim, Garmisch-Partenkirchen, Mittenwald, Kempten, Lindau and Augsburg.

Restaurants

Hotel restaurants

see Hotels

Top restaurants

*Aubergine, Maximiliansplatz 5
*Boettner, Theatinerstrasse 8
*Käferschenke, Schumannstrasse 1
*Maximilianstuben, Maximilianstrasse 27
*Sabitzer, Reitmorstrasse 21
*Tantris, Johann-Fichte-Strasse 7

Other Munich restaurants

Altes Hackerhaus, Sendlinger Strasse 75
Augustiner-Grossgaststätten, Neuhauser Strasse 16
Bratwurst-Herzl, Heiliggeiststrasse 3, Viktualienmarkt
Dallmayr, Dienerstrasse 14
Das Kleine Restaurant, Landsberger Strasse 315
Donisl, Weinstrasse 1 (Marienplatz; a typical old Munich restaurant in the former Guard-House)
Franziskaner, Residenzstrasse 9 (various different rooms – Brotzeitstüberl, Fuchsenstube, Klause, Schwemme; breakfast, morning drinks)
Grüne Gans, Am Einlass 5
Haxnbauer, Münzstrasse 2 (near Hofbräuhaus; specialties knuckle of calf and pork)
Hofbräuhaus, Platzl 9 (with Schwemme, country-style rooms on first floor, banqueting hall, garden; brass band plays daily)
Mathäser-Bierstadt, Bayerstrasse 5 (with Schwemme, other rooms, beer-garden, terraces)
Mövenpick, in Künstlerhaus, Lenbachplatz 8
Nürnberger Bratwurstglöckl, Frauenplatz 9
Olymp, in Olympic Tower, Spiridon-Louis-Ring 7 (revolving restaurant at 182 m/598 ft)
Peterhof, Marienplatz 22 (specialty weisswürste)
Platz, Münzstrasse 8 (folk shows in the evenings)
Ratskeller, in Rathaus, Marienplatz (entrance Marienplatz and Dienerstrasse)
Spatenhaus, Residenzstrasse 12
Spatenhof, Neuhauser Strasse 26
Zum Spöckmeier, Rosenstrasse 9 (near Marienplatz; an old-established Munich restaurant with panelled rooms)
Weisses Bräuhaus, Tal 10 (excellent weissbier)

Wine-houses

Feldherrnkeller, Theatinerstrasse 27
Hahnhof, Leopoldstrasse 32
Pfälzer Weinprobierstuben, in Residenz (entrance Residenzstrasse 1)
*Schwarzwälder's Naturweinhaus, Hartmannstrasse 8
Südtiroler Torggelstuben, Platzl 6
Weinkellet St. Michael, Neuhauser Strasse 11 (snack buffet, schrammelmusik)
Weinstadl, Burgstrasse 5

Balkan

Csarda Piroschka, Haus der Kunst, Prinzregentenstrasse 1
K.u.K. Monarchie, Reichenbachstrasse 22 (near Gärtnerplatz)
Makarska-Grill, Schleissheimer Strasse 182

Bohemian

Goldene Stadt, Oberanger 44
Praha, Rossmarkt 3
St Wenzel, Ungererstrasse 67

Chinese

Canton, Theresienstrasse 49
Haus Ming, Schwanthalerstrasse 7
Tai Tung, Prinzregentenstrasse 60

French

Austern-Keller, Römerstrasse 15
Bistro Terrine, Amalienstrasse 89 (Amalienpassage)
Bouillabaisse, Falkenturmstrasse 10
La Mer, Schraudolphstrasse 24
*Le Gourmet, Ligsalzstrasse 46
Savarin, Schellingstrasse 122
Werneckhof, Werneckstrasse 11

The Sendlinger Tor – included in every city tour

Greek

Akropolis, Rosenheimer Strasse 13A
Mykonos, Georgenstrasse 105
Olympia, Kellerstrasse 29

Italian

Bei Mario, Luisenstrasse 47 and Adalbertstrasse 15
Bologna, Leopoldstrasse 23
Da Pippo, Mühlbaurstrasse 36
Romagna Antica, Elisabethstrasse 52
*El Toula, Sparkassenstrasse 5
Osteria Italiana Lombardi, Schellingstrasse 62

Swiss

Chesa Rüegg, Wurzerstrasse 18
Walliser Stuben, Leopoldstrasse 33

Yugoslav

Opatija, Brienner Strasse 41
Stengelhof, Stengelstrasse 2

Sightseeing tours

City tours are run by Münchner Fremden-Rundfahrten OHG; office in Central Station, tel. 59 04-2 48
Departures from Bahnhofplatz (opposite main entrance to station)

Short tour

Daily at 10 and 11.30 a.m. and 2.30 p.m. (1 hour)

Extended short tour

Daily at 10 a.m. and 2.30 p.m. (including Olympic Park and Olympic Tower; $2\frac{1}{2}$ hours)

Longer tour (2½ hours)

Daily, except Mon., at 10 a.m.: including Frauenkirche and Alte Pinakothek
Daily, except Mon., at 2.30 p.m.: including Nymphenburg Palace and Treasury of Residenz (on Sun. only Nymphenburg and Amalienburg)

Munich by night

Daily, except Sun., at 7.30 p.m. (about 5 hours)

Towers (viewpoints)

See that entry

Souvenirs

The most popular souvenir of Munich is a *masskrug* (litre tankard), more than 200,000 of which disappear every year from beer-halls, beer-gardens and beer-tents.
Shops selling Bavarian souvenirs, of varying degrees of genuineness and originality, are to be found around the Hofbräuhaus, in the pedestrian zone, in the Stachus underground shopping centre and in the Central Station.

Specialist shops

Well-known specialist shops:

Beck am Rathauseck,
Marienplatz 11, tel. 2 36 91-0
Textiles

Alois Dallmayr,
Dienerstrasse 14, tel. 21 35-0
Delicatessen, freshly roasted coffee

Heinrich Hugendubel,
Salvatorplatz 2, tel. 23 89-1
Books (also bookstore at Marienplatz 22)

Feinkost-Käfer,
Prinzregentenstrasse 73, tel. 41 68-1
Delicatessen

Sport-Scheck,
Sendlinger Strasse 85, tel. 21 66-1
Sports goods

Sport-Schuster,
Rosenstrasse 5, tel. 2 37 07-0
Sports goods

Sport

Information

The Municipal Sports Office (Städtisches Sportamt) provides information about sports and sports facilities in the various sports clubs (tel. 2 33/62 24) and the city's programme of leisure sporting activities (tel. 2 33/87 15).

Leisure Centre for Health

Under the west stands of the Olympic Stadium in Spiridon-Louis-Ring is the Leisure Centre for Health (Freizeitzentrum zur Gesunderhaltung), run jointly by the city and the Volkshochschule (Adult Education Centre). Here every day there is a full programme of sporting, psychological and creativity-stimulating events, open to all without prior appointment.
Information: tel. 30 20 07.

Keep-fit trails (Trimm-dich-Pfade)

Feldmochinger See (off Karlsfelder Strasse)
Forstenrieder Park (south of Neuried, off Parkstrasse)
Isaranlagen (north of Hellabrunn Zoo, on Alemannenstrasse)
Kapuzinerhölzl (north of Botanic Gardens, In den Kirschen)
Perlacher Forst (at south end of Oberbiberger Strasse; State Forestry Department and Municipal Park Department)
Sendlinger Wald (South Park, off Inninger Strasse)
Wasserbogengelände (south side of Pasing Municipal Park, on B 12)

Tennis

There are tennis courts in various parts of the city which can be hired by the hour (managed by Sport-Scheck KG).
Information and booking: tel. 21 66-1

Swimming

See Swimming-pools

Skating

The Ice Stadium in the Olympic Park (see A to Z) is open throughout the year. Skates can be hired.
Information on opening times: tel. 38 64/2 35.

Sports stadiums

Olympic Stadium,
Olympic Park
U-Bahn: Olympiazentrum
Open (sightseeing visits): daily 8 a.m.–6 p.m. (April–September) and 9 a.m.–4 p.m. (October to March)
Advance booking of tickets: see Ticket agencies
Seating for 78,000. The venue of important football matches

Olympic Cycling Stadium,
Olympic Park
U-Bahn: Olympiazentrum
Advance booking of tickets: see Ticket agencies

Ice Stadium,
Olympic Park
U-Bahn: Olympiazentrum
Advance booking of tickets: see Ticket agencies
Ice-hockey matches

Stadion an der Grünwalder Strasse,
Grünwalder Strasse 4
U-Bahn: Silberhornstrasse
Trams: 15, 25
Bus: 51
Football matches

Dantestadion,
Dantestrasse 14

The tent-roofed Olympic stadiums

Trams: 15, 20, 25
Field and track events

Prinzregentenstadion,
Prinzregentenstrasse 80
Tram: 18
Bus: 55
Ice sports

Swimming pools

Open-air pools

The municipal open-air pools are open daily May to September from 8 a.m. to 7 or 7.30 p.m.

Dantebad,
Dantestrasse 6, tel. 15 28 74
Trams: 15, 20, 25
Buses: 83, 177
Stadium with stand for spectators, 5 pools, diving-pool with 10 m (33 ft) high tower
Extensive sunbathing lawns

Georgenschwaige,
Belgradstrasse 195, tel. 30 99 13
U-Bahn: Scheidplatz

Maria Einsiedel,
Zentralländstrasse 28, tel. 7 23 14 01
Quiet, with trees

Michaelibad,
Heinrich-Wieland-Strasse 16, tel. 40 76 91
U-Bahn: Michaelibad
To the east of the city. Five pools, diving pool with 10 m (33 ft) high tower, extensive sunbathing lawns

Schyrenbad,
Claude-Lorrain-Strasse 24, tel. 65 37 15
U-Bahn: Kolumbusplatz
Bus: 58

Ungererbad,
Traubestrasse 3, tel. 36 98 42
U-Bahn: Dietlindenstrasse
In northern Schwabing; popular with students

Westbad,
Weinbergerstrasse 11, tel. 88 54 41
Tram: 19
In a beautiful park; popular with families. Naturist area for women only.

Sommerbad Allach,
Eversbuschstrasse 213, tel. 8 12 54 27
S-Bahn: Karlsfeld
Bus: 75

Prinzregentenbad,
Prinzregentenstrasse 80, tel. 47 48 08
Tram: 18
Buses: 51, 54, 55
Swimming-pool, sports pool, children's paddling-pool; inadequate sunbathing area

Floriansmühle,
Floriansmühlstrasse 23, tel. 32 55 22
Buses: 290, 292, 691

Other bathing-places in summer

There is good bathing in the Isar and the Eisbach in the Englischer Garten (but not on the lake). The Isar is suitable for bathing from the southern city boundary to the Reichenbachbrücke and from the Prinzregentenbrücke to the Kennedybrücke (with interruptions). The stretch near the Flauchersteg is particularly popular.

Covered pools

Dante-Warmfreibad,
Postillonstrasse 17, tel. 15 28 74
Trams: 15, 20, 25
Pool open Oct.–Apr., Sat.–Mon. 9 a.m.–5.30 p.m., Tue.–Fri. 11 a.m.–8.30 p.m.
Sauna open all year round

Cosima-Wellenhallenbad,
Cosimastrasse 5, tel. 91 17 90
Buses: 89, 189
Open Mon. 4–8 p.m., Wed. and Fri. 8 a.m.–8 p.m., Tue. and Thu. 7 a.m.–8 p.m., Sat. 8 a.m.–5 p.m., Sun. and pub. hol. 7.30 a.m.–5 p.m.
Water heated Tue. and Thu.
Artificial waves Mon.–Fri. from 4 p.m., Sat., Sun. and pub. hol.

at full hours and half-hours
Sauna, outdoor pool with bubbling warm water, sunbathing lawn

Olympic Swimming Hall,
Olympic Park, tel. 3 86 43 90
U-Bahn: Olympiazentrum
Open daily 7 a.m.–9.30 p.m. (Mon. from 10 a.m.)
Swimming-pool, sauna

Forstenrieder Park,
Stäblistrasse 27B, tel. 75 60 57
Buses: 64, 65
Open Mon. 10 a.m.–5 p.m., Tue. and Thu. 7 a.m.–7.45 p.m., Wed. and Fri. 8 a.m.–7 p.m., Sat. 8 a.m.–5 p.m., Sun. 7.30–11.30 a.m.
Water heated Tue. and Thu.
Swimming-pool, sauna

Giesing-Harlaching,
Klausener Strasse 22, tel. 6 92 55 17
Trams: 15, 25
Bus: 51
Open Mon. 10 a.m.–5 p.m., Tue. and Thu. 7 a.m.–7.45 p.m., Wed. and Fri. 8 a.m.–7 p.m., Sat. 8 a.m.–5 p.m., Sun. and pub. hol. 7.30 a.m.–5 p.m.
Water heated Tue. and Thu.

Michaelibad,
Heinrich-Wieland-Strasse 24, tel. 40 76 91
U-Bahn: Michaelibad
Open Mon. 10 a.m.–5 p.m., Tue. and Thu. 7 a.m.–7.45 p.m., Wed. and Fri. 8 a.m.–7 p.m., Sat. 8 a.m.–5 p.m.
Closed Sundays in July and August
Water heated Tue. and Thu.
Swimming-pool, sauna

Westbad,
Weinbergerstrasse 11, tel. 88 54 41
Tram: 19
Open Tue. and Thu. 7 a.m.–7.45 p.m., Wed. and Fri. 7 a.m.–6.30 p.m., Sat. 8 a.m.–5 p.m., Sun. 7.30–11.30 a.m.
Closed Sundays in July and August
Water heated Mon. and Fri.
Swimming-pool, sauna, individual baths, showers

Südbad,
Valleystrasse 37, tel. 76 15 69
U-Bahn and S-Bahn: Harras
Open Mon. 10 a.m.–4 p.m., Tue. and Thu. 8 a.m.–7.45 p.m., Wed. and Fri. 8 a.m.–6.30 p.m., Sat. 8 a.m.–5 p.m., Sun. 7.30–11.30 a.m.
Water heated Mon. and Thu.

Nordbad,
Schleissheimer Strasse 142, tel. 18 00 91
Open Mon. 10 a.m.–4 p.m., Tue.–Thu. 8 a.m.–6.30 p.m., Fri. 8 a.m.–7.45 p.m., Sat. 8 a.m.–5 p.m., Sun. 7.30–11.30 a.m.

Müllersches Volksbad,
Rosenheimer Strasse 1 (Ludwigsbrücke), tel. 4 48 32 20
S-Bahn: Isartor
Open Mon. 10 a.m.–6 p.m., Tue. and Thu. 8 a.m.–6.30 p.m., Wed. 6.45 a.m.–6.30 p.m., Fri. 8 a.m.–7.45 p.m., Sat. 8 a.m.–5 p.m., 5–8 p.m. (naturists)
Closed Sundays in July and August
Water heated Wed. and Fri.
Family pool and separate ladies' pool, medical baths (by appointment), Turkish baths, individual baths, showers

Taxis

Taxis can be called by telephone to any address in the city: tel. 21 61-1.
The telephone numbers of taxi ranks are listed on the inside front cover of the telephone directory.

Television

See Radio and television

Theatres

Bayerisches Staatsschauspiel (Residenztheater)
U-Bahn: Odeonsplatz
S-Bahn: Marienplatz
Advance booking: Max-Joseph-Platz 1, tel. 22 57 54. Open Mon.–Fri. 10 a.m.–12.30 p.m. and 3.30–5.30 p.m., Sat. 10 a.m.–12.30 p.m. Booking from Sat. for following Wed.–Tue.
Ticket office opens an hour before the performance

Altes Residenztheater
(see A to Z, Cuvilliés Theatre)
U-Bahn: Odeonsplatz
S-Bahn: Marienplatz
Advance booking: at Bayerische Staatsoper, Maximilianstrasse 11, tel. 22 13 16. Open Mon.–Fri. 10 a.m.–12.30 p.m. and 3.30–5.30 p.m., Sat. 10 a.m.–12.30 p.m.
Booking from 7 days before performance
Ticket office opens an hour before the performance

Theater am Marstall,
Marstallplatz 1
U-Bahn and S-Bahn: Marienplatz
Advance booking: at Bayerisches Staatsschauspiel
Mainly productions of Bayerisches Staatsschauspiel, but also of Bayerische Staatsoper

Münchner Kammerspiele im Schauspielhaus
(see A to Z, Kammerspiele)
U-Bahn and S-Bahn: Marienplatz
Advance booking: Maximilianstrasse 26, tel. 23 73 13 28. Open Mon.–Fri. 10 a.m.–6 p.m., Sat. and Sun. 10 a.m.–1 p.m. Booking from Sat. for following Tue.–Mon.

Werkraumtheater,
Hildegardstrasse 1
U-Bahn and S-Bahn: Marienplatz
Advance booking: at Münchner Kammerspiele
Productions by Münchner Kammerspiele

Kleine Komödie im Bayerischen Hof,
Promenadeplatz 6 (Hotel Bayerischer Hof), tel. 29 28 10
U-Bahn and S-Bahn: Marienplatz
Trams: 14, 19
Advance booking: Mon.–Sat. 11 a.m.–7 p.m., Sun. 3–6 p.m.
International light theatre

Kleine Komödie am Max-II-Denkmal,
Maximilianstrasse 47, tel. 22 18 59
S-Bahn: Isartor
Trams: 14, 19, 20
Bus: 53
Advance booking: Mon.–Sat. 11 a.m.–7 p.m., Sun. 3–7 p.m.

Deutsches Theater,
Schwanthalerstrasse 13, tel. 59 34 27
U-Bahn: Hauptbahnhof
S-Bahn: Karlsplatz
Advance booking: Mon.–Sat. 10 a.m.–2 p.m. and 3–6 p.m.
Germany's largest private theatre; operettas, singspiels, musicals; guest productions by world-famous companies

T(h)eater in der Brienner Strasse,
Brienner Strasse 50, tel. 52 19 07
U-Bahn: Königsplatz
Advance booking: Mon.–Sat. 11 a.m.–7 p.m.
Musicals, cabarets, concerts; no resident company

Theater "Die kleine Freiheit",
Maximilianstrasse 31 (Maximilianpassage), tel. 22 11 23
U-Bahn and S-Bahn: Marienplatz
Trams: 14, 19
Advance booking: Mon.–Sat. from 11 a.m., Sun. from 2 p.m.

Modernes Theater,
Hans-Sachs-Strasse 12, tel. 26 68 21
U-Bahn: Sendlinger-Tor-Platz, Fraunhoferstrasse
Advance booking: daily, except Mon., 4–6.30 p.m.,
tel. 22 54 73

TAMS – Theater am Sozialamt,
Haimhauserstrasse 13a, tel. 34 58 90
U-Bahn: Münchener Freiheit
Advance booking: by telephone, Tue.–Sat. from 3 p.m.
Critical and experimental theatre

Theater am Einlass,
Am Einlass 4 (Reichenbachplatz), tel. 2 60 82 80
U-Bahn and S-Bahn: Marienplatz
Advance booking: daily 10 a.m.–midday and 6–8 p.m.

Theater 44,
Hohenzollernstrasse 20, tel. 32 87 48
U-Bahn: Giselastrasse

Bus: 33
Advance booking: by telephone, daily, except Sun. and Mon., from 4 p.m.
Schwabing's oldest cellar theatre

Theater im Westend,
Guldeinstrasse 47, tel. 50 79 70
Trams: 19, 29
Buses: 32, 33
Advance booking: by telephone, daily 2–7 p.m.

KTM – Neues Münchner Künstlertheater,
Dachauer Strasse 112, tel. 18 42 43
Trams: 12, 20
Bus: 33
Ticket office open 7 p.m.

proT – Prozessions-Theater,
Isabellastrasse 40
U-Bahn: Hohenzollernplatz
Trams: 12, 18
Bus: 33
Advance booking: tel. 2 71 41 62

Off-Off-Theater,
Potsdamer Strasse 13
U-Bahn: Dietlindenstrasse
Buses: 43, 44, 85
Experimental theatre, with theatre for children and young people

theater k – Theater in der Kurfürstenstrasse,
Kurfürstenstrasse 8, tel. 33 39 33
U-Bahn: Universität
Trams: 12, 18
Bus: 33
Advance booking: from 5 p.m.

studiotheater München,
Ungererstrasse 19 (Fuchsbau)
U-Bahn: Münchener Freiheit
Advance booking: daily from 11 a.m., tel. 34 38 27 and 34 38 86

Theater in der Leopoldstrasse,
Leopoldstrasse 17, tel. 39 40 81
U-Bahn: Giselastrasse
Tickets from see Ticket agencies and theatre ticket office
No resident company

Theater Piccola Bavaria (Künstlerhaus),
Lenbachplatz 8, tel. 59 80 36
S-Bahn: Karlsplatz
Little theatre; modern plays

Theater im Weinhaus über dem Landtag,
Maria-Theresia-Strasse 2a, tel. 47 91 18 (from 6 p.m.)
Tram: 18
Buses: 51, 53

Theater Rechts der Isar,
Wörthstrasse 9, tel. 8 34 91 34, from 6 p.m. 4 48 36 57
S-Bahn: Ostbahnhof, Rosenheimer Platz

Theater der Jugend in der Schauburg,
Franz-Joseph-Strasse 47, tel. 2 37 21-3 65
Tram: 18
U-Bahn: Giselastrasse, Josephsplatz
Advance booking: Tue.–Sat. 2–6 p.m., for schools Mon.–Fri. from 9 a.m., tel. 2 37 21-3 63

Münchner Marionettentheater (Puppet Theatre),
Blumenstrasse 29a, tel. 26 57 12
U-Bahn: Sendlinger-Tor-Platz
Advance booking: Wed.–Sat. 10 a.m.–midday and 2–4.30 p.m., Sun. 10 a.m.–3 p.m.

Platzl,
Am Platzl (opposite Hofbräuhaus), tel. 29 31 01-5
U-Bahn and S-Bahn: Marienplatz
Folk and country singers

Cabarets

Song Parnass,
Einsteinstrasse 42, tel. 4 70 29 95

Schwabinger Brettl,
Occamstrasse 11, tel. 34 72 89

Liederbühne Robinson,
Dreimühlenstrasse 33, tel. 77 22 68

Drehleier,
Balanstrasse 23, tel. 48 43 37

Theater bei Heppel & Ettlich,
Kaiserstrasse 67, tel. 34 93 59

Ticket agencies

Tickets for theatres, concerts and other events (including events in the Olympic Park) can be obtained from the following ticket agencies. It should be noted that tickets for the Bavarian State theatres (National Theatre, Residenz Theatre, Gärtnerplatz Theatre) and the Kammerspiele can be obtained only from their own advance booking offices.

Abendzeitung-Schalterhalle,
Sendlinger Strasse 79, tel. 23 77-2 23

abr-Theaterkasse
Stachus (Karlsplatz), entrance in Sonnenstrasse,
tel. 59 04-4 19

Otto Bauer,
Landschaftstrasse (back of New Town Hall),
tel. 22 17 57
Tickets for concerts

Buchhandlung Lehmkuhl,
Leopoldstrasse 45, tel. 39 80 42
Open Mon.–Fri. 10 a.m.–6.30 p.m., Sat. 10 a.m.–1 p.m.
Tickets for concerts

Max Hieber,
Liebfrauenstrasse 1, tel. 22 65 71
Tickets for theatres and concerts

Radio-RIM,
Theatinerstrasse 17, tel. 22 65 03
Tickets for theatres and concerts

Residenz-Bücherstube,
Residenzstrasse 1 (in Residenz, opposite Feldherrnhalle),
tel. 22 08 68
Tickets for concerts

Hallo-Reiseservice im PEP,
Thomas-Dehler-Strasse 12, tel. 6 37 10 44

Studiosus-Reisen,
Amalienstrasse 73, tel. 28 07 68
For holders of student card only

tz München,
tel. 53 06-0

Ice Stadium, Olympic Park,
tel. 38 64-5 77
Open Mon.–Thu. 8 a.m.–5 p.m., Fri. 8 a.m.–2 p.m.
All events in Olympic Park (football, sporting events, concerts)

Advance booking for events in Olympic Park also at:
abr Stachus (see above)
abr Sendlinger Strasse 70, tel. 59 04–4 39
abr Hauptbahnhof, tel. 59 04-0
abr Pasing, in Pasing Station, tel. 83 80 75
Sport-Scheck, Sendlinger Strasse 85, tel. 21 66-1

For opera and ballet

See Music

For theatres

See Theatres

Towers (viewpoints)

Town Hall Tower (85 m (279 ft)),
New Town Hall, Marienplatz
Open Mon.–Fri. 8 a.m.–3.45 p.m., Sat., Sun. and pub. hol. 10 a.m.–6 p.m.

"Alter Peter" (99 m (325 ft)),
Rindermarkt (near Marienplatz)
Open Mon.–Sat. 9 a.m.–5 p.m., Sun. 10 a.m.–5 p.m.

South Tower of Frauenkirche (99 m (325 ft)),
Frauenplatz
Open in summer 8.30 a.m.–7 p.m., winter 9 a.m.–6 p.m.; lift

Olympic Tower (290 m (951 ft)),
Olympic Park
U-Bahn: Olympiazentrum
Open daily 8 a.m.–midnight (last admission 11.30 p.m.); parking

Trade fairs

Information about trade fairs in Munich can be obtained from the Munich Trade Fair and Exhibition Company (Münchener Messe- und Ausstellungsgesellschaft, MGG), Theresienhöhe 13, tel. 51 07-0.

Travel agencies

The more exclusive travel agencies, handling individual business and holiday travel, are to be found in the city centre. The travel departments of the large department stores and the Official Bavarian Travel Bureau (Amtliches Bayerisches Reisebüro, abr) deal mainly in package tours. Young people, 'back-packers' and modern-day globetrotters will find reasonably priced travel arrangements in the travel agencies in the University quarter (Amalienstrasse, Türkenstrasse).

What's on in Munich

"Official Monthly Programme"

The "Official Monthly Programme" published by the City Tourist Office (Offizielles Monatsprogramm des Fremdenverkehrsamtes München) contains up-to-date information about exhibitions, theatres and concerts, congresses and conferences, museums and galleries, together with a list of hotels, giving number of beds, tariff and amenities.

"Monthly Programme of the Olympic Park"

The "Monthly Programme of the Olympic Park" (Monatsprogramm Olympiapark München), obtainable from the Tourist Office and ticket agencies, gives information about sporting events, recreational facilities, conducted tours and sightseeing visits in the Olympic Park.

Youth hostels and guest-houses for young people

Young people can find reasonably priced accommodation in youth hostels and young people's guest-houses.
Since large numbers of young people, both German and foreigners, go to Munich during the summer months it is advisable to book well in advance. Bookings should be made direct with the youth hostel or guest-house: the Tourist Office is not able to make bookings in these establishments.
Information: Jugend-Informations-Zentrum (Youth Information Centre), tel. 53 16 55.

DJH Jugendherberge,
Wendl-Dietrich-Strasse 20, tel. 13 11 56
U-Bahn: Rotkreuzplatz
Bus: 83
Open: midday–11.30 p.m.
535 beds

DJH Burg Schwaneck,
Burgweg 4-6, 8023 Pullach, tel. 7 93 06 43
Open: midday–1 a.m.
131 beds; sports facilities

DJH Jugendgästehaus Thalkirchen,
Miesingstrasse 4, tel. 7 23 65 50/60
Buses: 31, 57
Open: midday–1 a.m.
346 beds; day rooms, discothèque, games rooms

Haus International/Jugendhotel,
Elisabethstrasse 87, tel. 18 50 81
420 beds; discothèque, swimming-pool, club rooms, leisure centre

CVJM (YMCA),
Landwehrstrasse 13, tel. 55 59 41
Near Central Station
Open all year round
80 beds; also takes girls

Jugendhotel für weibliche Jugendliche,
Goethestrasse 9, tel. 55 58 91
U-Bahn and S-Bahn: Hauptbahnhof
Open until midnight
30 beds; girls only

Jugendlager Kapuzinerhölzl,
Franz-Schrank-Strasse 8, tel. 1 41 43 00
Trams: 12, 41
Open end June to end August
Sleeps 400 in a large tent
No advance booking

Sportschule Grünwald,
Ebertstrasse 1, 8022 Grünwald, tel. 64 96 26
Tram: 25 from Sendlinger Tor
220 beds; advance written application necessary

Useful Telephone Numbers

Emergencies	
Police	2 14-1
Assault or traffic accident	1 10
Rescue service, first aid	22 26 66
Fire	1 12
Medical emergency service	55 86 61
Chemists – out-of-hours service	59 44 75
Breakdown assistance:	
ACE (Auto Club Europa)	53 65 02
ADAC (Allgemeiner Deutscher Automobil-Club	76 76 76
Information	
Tourist Office, Central Station	23 91 2 56 and 2 57
Tourist Office, Airport	23 91 2 66
Flight information	92 11 21 27
Youth Information Centre	53 16 55
Pilot stations:	
Freimann (Nürnberg motorway)	32 54 17
Ramersdorf (Salzburg motorway)	67 27 55
Unterdill (Garmisch motorway)	75 63 30
Obermenzing (Stuttgart motorway)	8 11 24 12
Airlines	
British Airways	29 11 21
Lufthansa	5 11 30
PanAm	55 81 71
Consulates	
United Kingdom	39 40 15
United States	2 30 11
Canada	55 85 31
Lost property offices	
Municipal	2 33-1
Railway (Central Station)	1 28 58 59
Railway (East Station)	12 88 44 09
Post Office	13 95 52
Motoring organisations	
ADAC (Allgemeiner Deutscher Automobil-Club	51 95-0
DTC (Deutscher Touring Club)	8 11 10 48
Taxis	21 61-1
Telegrams: to dictate on telephone	1 13
Telephone	
Services	1 14
Directory enquiries, inland	11 88
Directory enquiries, international	0 01 18
Exchange for international calls	00 10
Dialling codes:	
to United Kingdom	00 44
to United States or Canada	00 1